EXISTENTIAL FOLKTALES

EXISTENTIAL FOLKTALES

Margaret Switzer

CAYUSE PRESS

Thanks to all my friends and colleagues who have helped me with inspiration and support along the way.

Published by: Cayuse Press
              P.O. Box 9086
              Berkeley, California 94709

ISBN: 0-933529-00-7
Library of Congress Catalog Card: 85-70818

Printed in the United States of America

10   9   8   7   6   5   4   3   2   1

PS
3569
W59
E95
1985

To Herb Wilner

TABLE OF CONTENTS

EXISTENTIAL FOLKTALES

THE GOOSE GIRL

Real Theme: Hysteria

No one really knows where the first folktales came from, as usual. Probably they travelled the same routes as the rest of civilization and, more interestingly, the same route as philosophy. Philosophy was the intellectual pursuit of the upper classes, and folktales of the lower classes. The ones we've been most influenced by in our lifetimes are those of the Brothers Grimm, Hans Christian Andersen, and the similar prudish 19th century writers and translators, who derived their versions from, among others, the racy 17th century authors, Charles Perrault and Marie Catherine d'Aulnoy. Earlier versions were naturally cruder and more violent than those we were told as children with industrialization's heightened symbolism. They were simple stories, to begin with, depicting reality; they were lessons in how to live and what it means.

In our own era folklore is an academic discipline. Experts in the field are Folklorists, who catalog and record every known version of every extant tale. Marxist and psychoanalytic criticism cannot explain the meaning of these tales. Existential criticism, which takes each story for itself, has the problem of dealing with the numerous distinct and separate versions, making interpretation, if not meaningless, then difficult. As history moves on, knowledge in the field must resort to acrimonious quanta, lubricious phenomenology, and sedulous epistemological analysis. Folklore and philosophy blend into one.

Octavia Travis, the "Goose Girl," is a perfect example of this merging of subjects. She herself was a Folklorist in 1950, on the island of Maui. She studied all the myths and legends of every civilization on earth, large or small, and she was an expert particularly in European folktales. Her story needs to be told in its true and factual version just because it's so violent, gruesome, and crude in the previous tellings. The mistaken identity in this story is one within Octavia herself: she enjoyed folklore, but she was a bit ashamed of being just a Folklorist, and she really coveted the socially upgrading subject of philosophy. She wished she could call herself a philosopher, but she was afraid she was doomed forever to be just a Folklorist.

Octavia was a princess, so to speak, though not in the 18th or 19th century way women were princesses. She was runner-up to Miss Honolulu when she was nineteen, and her mother was so proud of her that she consented for Octavia to be married to the king of the pineapple industry in the islands, Frank Parsons, who lived at this time on Maui.

Several important details need to be explained about this tale, at least from the Grimms' version. They were a bit strange about pathetic fallacy and about attributing magical qualities to things. They told of a magic horse, named not Falada, but in reality Pierre and of three talking drops of blood, a sacrifice from Octavia's mother who pricked her finger with a non-magical needle just for the occasion. These three drops of blood had a name, too. It was Geraldine. As we all know from the psychoanalytic critics, the drops are in the story to signify menstrual blood, though in an interview for *U.S. News and World Report*, Geraldine denied having only a particular female function and purported to be symbolic of all blood in general.

Geraldine was on a handkerchief while Octavia rode Pierre to the ranch of Frank Parsons, accompanied by Gertrude, an assistant hired by Octavia's mother. Gertrude is in some ways the real main character of this story, since in reality she was called *Gertrude the Goose* for the way she walked, and for her rather long neck which made her not unpretty head stick out a bit. Because of the ridicule she had always been forced to endure from her peers, she had developed a persecution complex and an inferiority complex. She covered this with brash and rude rebelliousness.

So, as we all know, the procession was on its way to Frank's when Octavia got thirsty and asked Gertrude to reach her up a bottle of Coca Cola from the bag of groceries Gertrude was carrying.

"Get it yourself," snapped Gertrude.

"But it's no trouble for you. All you have to do is reach in the bag and grab it and hand it up to me," said Octavia. "You won't miss a step."

"I'm not your slave," growled Gertrude.

Octavia returned, "No, you're not my slave." After all, slavery had been outlawed for nearly a century. "You're my assistant, of course. You were hired to help me."

"Get off your horse and do it yourself."

So Octavia had to stop Pierre, dismount, reach into the bag, get a coke, mount up again, pop the top off on the saddle horn, and then, though the coke was a bit fizzy from being jostled around while they walked, she was finally able to quench her thirst.

3

Geraldine, wrapped in a piece of waxed paper so she wouldn't stain Octavia's clothes or dry out, called out in a shocked voice, "What if your mother found out she was paying an assistant who was so insubordinate?"

Octavia ignored the question. Soon after finishing the 6½ ounce bottle, and having put it in her saddle bag since Gertrude wouldn't take the empty back, she was again thirsty.

"Come on, Gertrude," she whined. "Just reach me up a bottle. It's no trouble. It's your job, for heaven's sake."

"That stuff is addictive," returned Gertrude. "I won't contribute to a drug addiction. Get it yourself."

Octavia again stopped Pierre, who'd been curiously silent, and got herself another bottle of coke. She had to listen to Geraldine's second shocked admonition, "What if your mother found out?" though she wasn't quite sure whether Geraldine meant Gertrude's insolence or the second bottle of Coca Cola, but then Gertrude stopped all attempts at resolving the issue by snatching Geraldine out of Octavia's pocket and throwing her off to the side of the road. Gertrude then forced the bag of groceries on the startled Octavia and mounted Pierre.

Gertrude had accomplished a significant role reversal here, and though she is in reality the main character in the story, everyone knows that Octavia, the beauty princess, is the one mistakenly paid the most attention by exegetes.

Octavia's problem, which no one has before correctly pointed out through ignorance, false modesty, or courtesy, was a form of paranoid hysteria. In fact, the most realistic critics theorize that the talking drops of blood and the talking horse were symptomatic hallucinations brought on by this hysteria. Further, they suggest that Gertrude did nothing wrong in this story, except be more interesting and attractive to Frank Parsons, the pineapple king, and Octavia's paranoia constructed the elaborate conspiracy plot which will now be explained correctly.

4

When they got to Frank's house, Gertrude was the one he fell for, for whatever reason: love is so peculiar. The deposed and dispossessed Octavia was forced to herd geese out in some distant corner of the ranch with an illiterate twerp named Conrad, who was always trying to pull her hair. The one time Octavia overheard Frank and Gertrude, the two lovers were having a discussion on lack of concretization in Kant's philosophy; Octavia could hardly conceptualize her envy and sorrow. All her desire to become a philosopher had to be sublimated. Some think this caused her to fantasize the talking horse, the talking drops of blood, even the expectation that Frank was supposed to want her.

The sensitive matter of Pierre must now be taken up. The violent and bloody Grimms' version has the horse beheaded as a safeguard by the usurping girl, and the horse head is then nailed up above a gate, where it chants rhymes whenever the goose girl passes. This century is certainly no less gruesome or violent than any other, but fidelity to the facts forces the truth to be told. Pierre was not beheaded, only taken out to the stable and kept there with his head hanging out over the top of the stall gate so that it just looked like he was a disembodied horse head. From there he did talk to anyone who came along, and that was often Octavia, once she found out where he was, but if you buy the hysteria explanation it was only a hallucination brought on by Octavia's hysteric paranoia.

At any rate, once he'd been incarcerated in the stall, Pierre hung his head over the door and said, "This is a pretty nice spread here though I'm not much for pineapples."

Jesse, the stable boy, was forking hay into the stalls. He was a good-looking dark fellow, part, but obviously not all, Hawaiian in descent. "Yeah," he said, "it's all right. Parsons is a good boss, but he's lonely for a family. He was instrumental in supplying the navy with pineapples during the war, you know.

5

He didn't make a dime himself off it. Wanted to help the war effort."

"Sounds like a good man," whinnied Pierre.

"Yeah, he is. He's good with horses, too," said Jesse. "He likes to take long rides in the morning, just as the sun rises."

"I'm not a morning individual," said Pierre. "I hope he has some other horses to take out."

"Sure he does. He's got everything here. It's a *family* he needs. I sure hope this marriage works out. He's been looking forward to it for so long."

Pierre discreetly kept his peace on the subject, out of loyalty. "Well," he thought, "I'm not really sure who I belong to now, between Gertrude and Octavia." He loved Octavia, but he had his job as a horse.

Inside the house, Frank and Gertrude were cozying up to each other over sloe gin fizzes, but out in the fields, overlooking a herd of geese, Octavia was contending with Conrad.

"Just leave me alone," she sobbed. "I'm not even supposed to be here. I'm supposed to be in there discussing ontology, epistemology, phenomenology, and metaphysics. Instead I'm out here like a common drudge, watching geese. Oh, Frank, why?"

"Frank who?" said the doltish and ugly Conrad, as he reached over behind her to grab her hair. "Come on, let's play games or something. How about telling some stories? I'll tell you how the Hawaiian Islands were formed. It was when some giants were slinging dirt clods at each other . . ."

Octavia's back arched in repulsion before he could even touch her, and she grabbed his hat off his head and threw it away, down into the wind so it flew a longer distance than anyone would think possible, thus giving rise to a teleportation theory in this story, at least concerning the hat. Of course the more pragmatic and psychoanalytical commentators explain it as a

6

symptom of hysteria, but somewhat defensively, with the recommendation Octavia give in to Conrad and just try to enjoy his quaint and folksy stories.

It didn't take too many rejections for Conrad to complain to Frank's son, Ron, that he couldn't get any attention from Octavia, and since it had been an unspoken agreement that she'd been obtained for Conrad's amusement, Ron had to try to get her to be more responsive. Ron was more Gertrude's and Octavia's age, something that should be suggestive of another subplot in this story, since the girls, either one, would have been better matched with him.

The important thing to remember in this story is not Octavia's alleged mental imbalance, defended by feminists as correctly felt anger nonconstructively used, but the bias and neglect always shown Gertrude, who is in reality the girl the tale is named for. Gertrude's presence in the Islands is accounted for by the fact that she had run away from home in Denver at the age of fourteen and hitched a ride to Portland, from where she stowed away on a merchant marine vessel. She jumped ship in Honolulu and spent several years working at any jobs she could find: waitress, office worker, babysitter, housekeeper.

She began to exhibit her persecution complex whenever anyone knocked on her door, or even stopped her in the street. She was afraid they were after her to send her back to Denver. Added to this was the slight physical deformity of being a bit duck-toed, and she felt she was too unattractive for any man to want. When Frank fell in love with her she was shocked but determined to keep him as her only hope for romance.

The final confrontation between Octavia and Gertrude occurred three years after the wedding of Frank and Gertrude. Octavia had stayed on to tend the geese in false confidence that her claim on Frank would be honored once the role reversal was discovered. She had to repel Conrad and avoid Ron all those years, while looking for her opportunity to catch Frank alone and explain the truth to him. Her only consolation and sustenance was to sneak into the stable to talk with Pierre about morality, first cause, and the status of science in the modern intellect.

One evening, though, when all the men were out at a stag party for another large rancher from the island, Gertrude interrupted the dialogue in the stable.

"So this is what happened to you," she said. "I've always wondered where you stumbled off to."

Octavia tried to hold in her bitterness, "You haven't wondered very hard. I've sent messages to Frank almost every day, informing him of the mix-up."

Gertrude laughed. "He never said a word about it to me."

"What could he have been thinking of? I took his silence as a cause for hopefulness."

"Oh, no!" gasped Gertrude.

"What?"

"He did mention it, but it didn't register to me that the crazy woman watching the geese was you. Oh, I am sorry!"

"So he knew I was here." Octavia was filled with an emotion half regret, half relief. She left the ranch that afternoon and lived the rest of her life with her mother in Honolulu.

THE HEN WHO BAKED THE BREAD

Real Theme: Positivism

Before the World Wars the world was a much different place, and undying optimism was considered by most normal people to be a desirable trait. In the last half of the twentieth century it has become an execrable trait. So it was hard for Thelma White to understand that her determination and pragmatism were a matter of ridicule in her town, where her mother and grandmother and great-grandmother had enjoyed the respect and admiration of the community. Thelma ran a bakery in North Platte, Nebraska. She specialized in freshly baked bread, but she also kept cakes and other sweets in the glass cases of her shop. In the back were her ovens and counters and storage cupboards, along with the big refrigerator where she kept eggs, butter, and milk.

People would walk by the shop and the smell of the pastries and bread would cause them to break their diets. The bakery had done a good business and had been open for sixty years, run by the maternal predecessors of Thelma. But before, there had been at least a mother and a daughter to run the business and get the baking done; when Thelma's mother died Thelma had to get hired help.

Thelma didn't really enjoy cooking. The dust-like flour made her sneeze and it was hard to stir and knead bread with her wings. She could if she had to, and she was quite good at it, but she just preferred other things: the bookkeeping, buying supplies, or handling the customers. So she wanted to hire a young man who would be the baker. She couldn't hire a journeyman because the union workers were too expensive. That left, as possibilities, young men on their first jobs, or drifters who were equally changeable and unreliable.

That didn't bother Thelma very much. She was a gregarious hen and along with the cheerful attitude she showed her customers, she had an equally positivistic outlook on life in general. It just didn't make sense to her for people to grumble or be melancholy. Every problem or setback she answered with "Oh, well, at least . . ." She looked on the bright side of everything and rarely lost her temper and never fell into despair. For this reason the townspeople laughed at her behind her back, and derisively mimicked her smiling sunny ways.

The first helper she had hired had been a college dropout named Carl. He was tall and energetic, and he sold drugs on the side, using his odd jobs as a cover since he'd been arrested before. His deals and connections used up so much of his time that he was almost always late to work. Thelma just thought he was forgetful, not knowing about his less moral pastimes. She even bought him a cheap wristwatch to help him keep track of the time. But before long special orders for wedding cakes and luncheon pastries backed up, and the bread sold out in the first hour because he hadn't baked enough. She regretfully let Carl go, apologizing to him many times and hoping for the best for his future and explaining how promptness was a necessity for holding a good job.

10

"I know you're a good boy, Carl," she told him, "and I like you and I hope for you to get a job somewhere else, but I know your mother and father well enough to know they would think I'm doing the right thing for you and for your future. I'm sorry if you were counting on this job for your survival, but you've just got to learn to be at work on time."

Confident that she would eventually find the right person for the job, she advertised again. The second helper was named Patrick. He was a little older, twenty-five, but he was an epileptic. Thelma knew that the disability could be overcome if only he were given a chance to perform. The human mind can overcome any obstacle if the will is strong enough. So she hired him and several seizures later she had to call him into her office for a talk.

"I know you can control this thing if only you try," she told him. "It's all in your mind. You think you'll have an attack, so you do. But if you want something badly enough, nothing, but nothing will stop you from getting it. Just make up your mind and when you feel an attack coming on, concentrate hard against it and repeat to yourself, over and over, 'No fit. No fit.'" She smiled her most sweet and encouraging smile and nodded as she looked right in his eyes.

"O.K.," he said. "But it seems like if I don't have one for a while, it builds up and the next one is worse."

"Don't be silly," she said.

It so happened that Patrick didn't have an attack for another month, and the bakery was just pulling up out of the down-swing it had been in when he finally did have one. In falling to the ground he spilled both the flour and the sugar bins and ruined much of the rest of the inventory. It was a very bad attack, and he severely burned himself on the oven before Thelma could quiet him and call for help. As the ambulance attendants lifted the exhausted man into the back of the ambulance, Thelma said to herself, "He must not have wanted *not* to have an attack, really. He could have controlled it if only he could have thought positively."

At this time she was being courted by Adam Mapes, who worked at the hardware store across the street. She was sure he was just waiting for the right moment to pop the question. Then, after the wedding, he would come to work with her, and as soon as the first egg arrived and she had to take time off to hatch it, he could run the bakery for her.

The night after Patrick's attack, Thelma and Adam went to the movies to see *An American In Paris*. Afterwards they walked home underneath the sycamore trees lining the sidewalk. He said to her, "You're having some real bad luck with hired help, aren't you?" His wingtip brushed lightly against hers.

"It's not luck, Adam," she said. "Things happen for a good reason in life. We make everything the way it is. Maybe I am at fault for not choosing the right person. But whatever I did, I thought it was the right thing at the time, so there's no harm done. I know everything is going to turn out all right."

Just telling him reinforced her positivity for her and she slept soundly that night. The next day the health inspector came for his yearly check, and since she hadn't had time to clean up the mess Patrick had made, he found the spilled flour and sugar under every appliance, and dirt and grease all over, since in trying to save the business, no one had had time to clean. The inspector ordered the place shut down immediately and he slapped a heavy fine on her. Thelma had to call the janitorial service she had used in the past. It took them an especially long time to get the job done since they knew how Thelma was. She refused to see anything but the good side of things, so while they were supposed to be scrubbing and mopping, they played poker and told her they were working as fast as they could. After a few days her feathers began to get a bit ruffled, but she didn't let it bother her.

The closure put the bakery even farther behind and alienated many of the usual customers, who were appalled at the thought they had been eating bread baked in such an unhygienic atmosphere. Thelma had to call her creditors and suppliers and talk them into another month of credit, which was easy for her because of her positive enthusiastic way on the telephone.

Looking at all the unpaid bills on her desk, she sighed. "Oh well," she reaffirmed to herself. "Everyone has difficulties, but what counts is how well we cope with them. It won't be long now before things turn around."

Once she had the bakery clean and open again, she began to interview prospective helpers, and she hired a young man named Sid, who had been in trouble with the law all his life, but who, Thelma knew, only needed someone to believe in him enough to help him get on the right road in life. She taught him how to make the bread dough and how to knead it and form the loaves. She taught him how to make perfect pastry. He was fairly attentive, but he did use obscene language so often she had to ask him not to. They soon had quite a good rapport going. Sid would tell her the stories of the ways he had defied authority in the past, and she would listen sympathetically and at the end of his stories say such things as "Well, that was a bad time for you, but now you've started over and you know better," and "It's not good to dwell on the past, but use your experiences as a rich source of wisdom," and "It's good that you have such a close understanding of misfortune: you can use it to avoid misfortune in the future."

Sid knew better than to listen to Thelma. He began stealing money from the cash register, and by the time she caught him he had brought the business to the edge of bankruptcy. She cornered him in the back room after closing time and confronted him with her evidence. He took a slicing knife from the table and held it to her throat while he raped her viciously. Then he emptied the cash register and her purse, and after laughing at

13

the paltry sum of money, he stole her car and took off for Wyoming.

She recovered her composure after a few minutes, feeling that she was lucky not to have been killed, and as she reached for the phone to call the authorities, it rang. It was someone from the bank that carried the loan on her car. They told her they were going to have to repossess it in the morning if she couldn't come up with the three late payments. That was out of the question, she said, she was broke, and she said she had just been robbed and besides the car had been stolen by the thief.

Then she dialed the police and told them to give the car to the bank if they ever recovered it. She locked up and went home, walking along the sidewalk lined with sycamores, and she went straight to sleep thinking, "It could be worse."

The next morning she was awakened by the phone. It was Patrick's lawyer, informing her that Pat was suing her for the injuries he had sustained from his last fit, and for the mental anguish he had gone through since then.

"He seems to think you are responsible for the severity of the attack. You had told him to restrain himself, and that inhibition made the seizure more severe."

She set her beak firmly. "He didn't try hard enough."

"His hospital bills are your responsibility."

"He can't sue me."

"How does a hundred thousand dollars sound?"

"You won't win. It's not right."

"I've already found a precedent. It's open and shut. I'd advise you to settle out of court."

"It'll wipe me out," she said.

"Tough luck," said the lawyer, who laughed and hung up.

Thelma sighed deeply but didn't give way to depression. She dialed Adam's number. "Could you come and pick me up?" she asked.

14

He arrived soon after she called, and she told him all the things that had happened to her.

"It's just destiny," he said. "Not even luck could account for all those disasters. It's just some dark hideous unexplainable force in the universe that has set itself to destroy you. Something both unpredictable and unknowable."

"Don't be an idiot," she snapped.

"I mean it. All we can do about it is recognize it. We can't change it. And eventually it does destroy us."

"There's nothing there that we aren't perfectly capable of knowing and controlling. And even if there were, I wouldn't dignify it with recognition."

"But it's so obvious. This can't have been just accident."

"Ultimately it doesn't matter. What we don't know, we have no business talking about."

Adam shook his head in disbelief and tried to return her smile. Then he dropped her off at the bakery.

"Will you pick me up tonight?" she asked.

"I don't think so," he said with a forced smile that showed his agony. "In fact, I think it's time we gave up trying to make our friendship work. The differences between us are irreconcilable. I can't go on with it."

"Nonsense," she said. "If we all said that no eggs would get hatched at all."

He looked past her. "Nevertheless," he said, "I want to call it off."

"If that's the way you feel about it, it's fine with me." She smiled sweetly at him to show there were no hard feelings.

Then he drove off and she walked up to her front door and unlocked it. She prepared the shop for opening time, even though the inventory was very low. There was a little flour left, so she started making the bread in the back room. While it was baking, she called her lawyer and told him about the lawsuit.

15

"That's ridiculous," he said. "You're not liable for a chronic disability."

"He said it was open and shut."

"That's just a technique to scare you. I say we fight it out. It might be a long bloody battle that lasts years, but they have no right to blame you because the man's an epileptic."

"That's the spirit," said Thelma. "Prepare a defense. I'm with you every step of the way."

Her faith in justice reaffirmed, she made another call, this one to the newspaper to run her ad for someone to help at the bakery.

GOLDILOCKS
AND THE THREE BEARS

Real Theme: Nothingness

Most people believe this story occurred once upon a time. This is, in fact, not quite the case. Goldilocks was a girl who lived in Tennessee in the mid-1950's. Her mother worked as a beautician, and seeing that her daughter was going to be a ravishing natural blonde, began grooming her for a Hollywood position to replace Marilyn Monroe, who would soon be of sentimental interest only. Goldilocks' mother, whose name was Susan, brushed those gold locks and dreamed of the day they would be worth millions and she could retire and never again have to smell setting lotion or perm gel. Susan's husband, Floyd, was a bit of a boozer and ruffian, and she longed to take her daughter and escape the threats of his violence and vulgarity.

Goldilocks' real name was Cassandra. She wanted to be called Casey, but at first everyone called her Sandy and then the detested "Goldilocks." She had always been a good and quiet child, perhaps a bit underactive, preferring to sit and stare into space rather than leap, run, or play vigorously with the other children.

Susan watched this, as the days went by, and wondered why, when she needed a dynamic, energetic, and vivacious blonde daughter to excite the movie audiences of the future, she had drawn such a deadbeat. This was no obstacle though, and while she shampooed and set the local ladies' hair, she would send her daughter out on errands to keep her busy and build her energy level. Every time Susan caught Goldilocks sitting staring blankly at a *Life* magazine or lolling about on the sofa gazing out the window, she sent her out for a walk to get some fresh air.

Goldilocks was easygoing. She did as she was told, not angrily or with resentment. In fact, not with any excitement at all, but with the attitude that rather than sit and think of nothing (which is what she did), while her mother who was herself dreaming, thought Goldilocks was daydreaming, she might as well go out and do something just to fill the void.

Goldilocks' was a case of the mind, fraught with dilemmas and paradoxes of existence, being caught and fixated on the abyss. One could argue with some validity that this was not the low-grade depression that afflicts much of the present-day population, but genuine high-grade depression. While Susan schemed and planned an early retirement with all the material possessions and sensual gratification the human appetite could desire, Goldilocks looked at it all as chains and barriers to some freedom she conceived as being full of mystery and rich with infinite delight. She despaired of ever finding this in any existent phenomenon and feared the vision itself was yet another empty illusion.

"Oh nothingness, nothingness," she could be heard muttering to herself on one of the many walks her mother sent her on, "to get air," as if all she experienced wasn't hollow and air-filled enough. "Nothingness all around me; nothingness in my past, nothingness in my future. It's all so empty, why *bother* being at all?"

Alas, the question itself was an empty one, and she never bothered posing it to anyone but herself, if such a thing as self existed, which she doubted, but found it difficult to prove or disprove. If there was anything, it would have to present itself to her on its own initiative, just as she considered life had done. *She* had had no choice in the matter.

Well, as always, the cabin appeared in the woods, as if some illusion were trying to become real, and she sighed in detached acceptance and entered it, thinking that to oppose fate would be a contradiction: it would be a positive distinct stand, a some-thing. It was nothing to her whether the house was there or not, whether she entered it or not, whether it was occupied or not. It was just another meaningless gesture.

The three bears had not left, as most people believe, to stroll until the soup cooled, but because Baby Bear had sliced his front paw badly while trying to cut the bread, even after Mama Bear had told him not to. He had wanted to feel a part of the providing process to counteract the degrading effects on his ego of dependency. Anyway, they had left in a hurry to take him to the emergency room to have the paw stitched up.

Goldilocks, as was previously stated, sighed deeply and went into the house. She looked at the front room with the fireplace in the corner, the chairs, the television which told her the bears were pretty well-off (since TV was just coming in), and the china cabinet full of knickknacks.

"What means we go to to fill the emptiness," she said.

She smelled the porridge and followed the smell back through a hallway and into the kitchen to the kitchen table. The kitchen was bright and sunny, with homemade checked curtains held back from the windows. It was a shiny clean kitchen and it depressed her to think of all the work someone had gone

19

to in keeping it so. But the porridge smelled good. She hesitated: even hunger was suspect. Maybe she was substituting filling her stomach for filling the void.

In any case, she sat down at the largest bowl, thinking that it would take that much to fill her abyss. It steamed like a hotspring, but she placidly stuck the edge of the stainless steel spoon into it and tasted. Ow! It burned her tongue, and she had to make that terrible decision of whether to be so vulgar as to spit it out or to swallow it, thus burning the remainder of her ingestive system. She spit it back into the bowl and smoothed it over with the spoon. No one would ever know.

Nursing her wounded tongue on the roof of her mouth, she half-heartedly moved to the middle seat. Ah, why? she asked herself. In spite of an urge to leave the question unanswered, she thought: Life is just a series of conscientiously entered experiments by man which end in injury. To bear pain with dignity was noble, if that mattered.

The second spoon was dipped into the second bowl with a certain self-loathing. "Bottomless pit of my hunger; bottomless pit of my hope." It, of course, was too cold. She considered eating it anyway, for self-flagellation, but instead she shrugged indifferently and moved to the smallest bowl.

The fact that the small bowl of porridge was at a palatable temperature was further illustration of the irony of life. She wouldn't be able to get full from such a small amount, but so what? She ate it quickly, tasting little.

Bored with food, she reentered the living room and threw herself into the biggest chair with the express intent of having herself a nice cry. But instead of sinking comfortably into the anticipated cushions, there were none and she landed somewhat surprised on the hard surface of a large wooden chair.

Feeling for bruises after the forced strenuous leap, she changed to the medium-sized chair. This one did have cushions and pillows, which sank underneath her as if full, or more accurately, half-full of feathers. That would be much too comfortable: not only would it give her a false sense of comfort, but also the feeling the chair was closing in around her. She heaved herself out of it with much effort and sat on the little straw child's chair. Her knees were too high so that her petticoat showed under her dress, but she didn't adjust it; no one was around.

She sat there with her elbow on her knee and her chin in her palm. Blonde hair hung all around her and she tried to push it back over her shoulders. She longed for the return of the days before she had discovered nothingness. Then: duty, rebellion, charity, fortune hunting, propagation of the species; anything but this terrible absence. Then she could play with dolls: after the knowledge, never again. That chasm, that rift between her dream of how existence was (baking cookies with Mommy and sitting on Daddy's lap watching TV, preferably cartoons), that void had stripped her of all attachments and pleasures, and once she realized how meaningless existence was she was paralyzed into a state of passive and depressed sighing.

Unable to muster tears in the dispassionate realization of the position she was living in and the simultaneous realization of the absurdity of it (as if she were forced to wear those horrible plastic sunglasses her mother had bought her, and had worn them just to be ridiculous like the world) she decided to explore the upstairs. On the stairway she stopped to look at the calendar. Days were circled and appointments were written in on some of the days. Whoever lived here was not consumed with emptiness. Would it be different for her when she grew up? Would she ever find something? Anything?

She got to the top of the stairs and stopped to rest. The second story was merely a loft with three beds, a dresser, and a wardrobe as a closet. Whoever lived here was not a privacy fanatic either, she concluded. Everything was open for all to see. All three beds were lined up against the wall.

Tired, oh so tired beyond her years, she laid her body on the largest bed. Ah, the loneliness of that vast expanse of bed! She felt like an amoeba in the ocean. It was terrifying.

She tried the middle bed. She didn't feel much better, maybe like a jellyfish in the ocean.

There was a night table between the two beds with a lamp and some books on it. One was on crocheting, and the other was a brief history of the Napoleonic Wars. She got out of bed and rummaged through the wardrobe and the dresser drawers inside it. Surely there would be something there. She didn't want to take it and make it her own; she simply wanted to find something, a proof of reality, a symbol of the meaning of existence. But, clothes, only clothes and an old photo album were in the closet.

So it was bears who inhabited this house. She noticed all the banal poses and shots included in the photo album, and she realized bears were just like everyone else. She replaced the album with despair, and threw herself on the last bed, her feet dangling slightly over the end. She contemplated the nothingness for a while, then fell asleep. She did not dream.

Now some accounts of this event have her being discovered by Baby Bear after the bears returned from the Emergency Room. This is known as the "Who's Been Sleeping In My Bed," or the "Identity Crisis" theory of this case.

Baby Bear, who was called Baby after his baby-face but who was really a quite advanced virile teenager, had arrived home while she was in the kitchen eating porridge and after his parents had decided to go out to lunch. He, after the blood and stitches, wasn't hungry any more. The two formal theories conflict as to whether he was already in the bed taking a nap or whether he was in the bathroom and arrived at the bed after Goldilocks was asleep.

22

There is no evidence for either, and these somewhat Marxist interpretations show Baby Bear trying to seduce Goldilocks to prove to her there is at least one thing worth living for, but this must be an ending contrived to lead the reader to a propagandistic moral. One suggestion is that Goldilocks rejected his advances with disinterest, and he, justifiably offended and hurt, demanded to know if she refused him because he was a bear.

It seems more likely that, considering her character, Goldilocks slept for an hour or two, then left fifteen minutes before the bears, who had had to wait for a long time at the busy emergency room, arrived home. She would have missed them, and undoubtedly, even if she *had* encountered them, would not have been able to relate to them anyway.

RUMPELSTILTSKIN

Real Theme: Identity Crisis

There was once, not a miller, but an old cardshark named Joe Barton, who lived in South Texas. It was 1957 when he found he was suffering from glaucoma. He had for many years supported himself and his beautiful daughter Winifred, so he had to figure out some way of making his abilities so valuable that rich men would hire him for consultations on betting techniques even after he had lost his sight. Towards this purpose he told a wealthy land baron and cattle rancher, Fulton Forbes, that Winifred was a good luck charm who brought big pots to whoever she stood near.

"It's her name, you see," Barton explained, hoping to get an in with Forbes and later become his consultant.

Forbes, a fat, overly sunburned short man, who perpetually chewed Big Hunk candy bars, said, "Sounds like something I could use. But before I'm convinced, I'm going to need some proof. Bring her to our blackjack game tonight and we'll test her out."

"We'll be there about eight," Joe said.

Forbes returned sourly, "I said her, not you."

Barton had always been disgusted with Forbes. Joe himself smoked cigars and had aged aesthetically, staying trim by playing tennis and keeping his white hair and mustache well-groomed. However, once he started he had no choice, so he sent Winnie to the ranch that night, by taxi-cab.

"Stand by me here, darlin', and bring me face cards," said Forbes, oozing delight at her slim waist, nice legs, and firm breasts that poked out a green sweater.

At the table were four other wealthy ranchers and land-owners. The game proceeded rapidly, with large stacks of red, white, and blue chips appearing, disappearing, and reappearing in front of each of the players.

The dealer was a slender, young, and handsome man with a serious and sensitive expression, very white skin and thick lips, and fine hair cut a little long. He wore tight levis and a dress cowboy shirt with a leather vest over it, and he dealt with talent and finesse, though no one talked to him or referred to him. He was like a nameless machine dispassionately responding to the requests of the wealthy old men and the rules of the game.

Forbes won and lost evenly for five hours; then he began to lose seriously.

"Fine good luck charm you are," he snapped at Winnie. He opened a fresh Big Hung and threw the crumpled brown wrapper near her feet.

Then, as if by magic, Forbes began to win big. Soon the other players were bored, discouraged, and tired, so they decided to quit playing and go home. Forbes told the handsome dealer to drive the girl back to her father's house, after giving her five thousand as a kind of commission.

In the blue Ford station wagon, once they left Forbes' property, the young man said, "I saved your ass, girl; how about giving me a split on that five grand?"

"Just how did you do that?"

"That old bag of stew meat was on a losing streak that had no end til I started dealing off the bottom. You'd have been out the door unless I tossed him the right cards."

"But that's dishonest," Winnie protested.

"So is tax fraud."

She ungrudgingly split the money. The next night Forbes called Joe and said he wanted to try her out on poker, so Joe called a taxi, and Winnie was soon out on the ranch standing by Fulton Forbes in his game room, this time wearing a low-cut, white blouse that showed some nice cleavage.

Again the dealer was the same young man, and this time Winnie watched carefully to try to tell when cards came off the bottom. When the game was over and Forbes had taken the money of the other players, Winnie and the dealer climbed into the station wagon to drive home, Winnie with ten grand this time. She was very aware of all the space inside the car and the smell of the ash tray.

"I suppose you're going to tell me you made him break the others again," she said, looking across the huge front seat at his dark silhouette.

"Sure did. I figure you owe me half. That's all." He turned the steering wheel with great gestures of his arms, as though it was a tremendous labor.

"But I didn't see you deal off the bottom."

"If you could see it, I wouldn't have a job."

Winnie thought to herself a minute then said, "And they don't pay a nickel of income tax?"

"Those fellows there tonight were all the state politicians in the area. How do you think these guys got rich?"

"Gambling?" Winnie wondered why her father had never made a fortune.

"No. They made a bunch of shady deals for land and bribed the lawmakers to make the values go up."

Something in it appealed to her sense of justice, so she split the ten thousand and felt slightly elated at being in the middle of a sting. But the next night Forbes came himself to pick her up, and the lust of greed was alive in him. "Craps," he said, cackling as they drove under the Double F brand arch over the entrance to the driveway of his house. "If you can do with dice what you do to the cards, I'm going to be the richest man in Texas."

Winnie said quietly, "I wonder if I *can* do with dice what I do with cards," but the comment went unnoticed.

When they entered the game room this time, Winnie saw the handsome dealer at the other end of the crap table and she sighed with relief when he looked at her and smiled.

She stood by Forbes as he threw the dice. The first roll was a seven, a winner. Then he threw a nine, which he matched after five more rolls. The other players placed chips on the table, and the mysterious dealer took the lost chips or paid the winning bets with a smooth rhythmical swinging of his arms and upper body, all the time with a slight smile on his lips.

No one else threw the dice all evening. Forbes was the designated roller—well, it *was* his house. The others managed to win or lose or break even on their bets, but somehow Forbes won nearly all the time. Even when he crapped out, it was when he had bet that he would. He lost a few chips on small bets on Big 6 or Big 8, or on the riskier long shots, but for the most part he won, and the chips piled up in front of him.

Winifred looked at the mysterious man who had helped her, or at least shared her earnings with her. She began to picture what it would be like to be held in his arms, to kiss him.

When the evening was over, the three of them were alone, drinking brandy in the leather chairs of the game room.

"Well, honey," said Forbes. "You certainly are everything your Daddy said you'd be."

27

"Oh," she said in a sing-song voice, feeling quite disgusted with herself, "I'm just me."

"You just got yourself some magical power, don't you? You got some kind of psychic knowledge or some kind of ESP, or whatever they call it."

"Oh, I don't know what it is."

Forbes set his Big Hunk in his empty brandy snifter and sat up in his large leather chair. "Well, you may or may not know that I was talking to your Daddy today. He owes me a few gambling debts don't nobody know about. And we made a deal: I promised to tear up his IOU's if he'd let you be my wife. How about that?"

Winifred was horrified but kept her wits. What had her father been thinking about? "Well, that sounds just delightful. Mistress of this whole ranch, just think."

The stranger had been silent all this time, but Winifred could feel his agitation at the proposition. She risked one look into his large green eyes and tried to plead to him.

He said, "Fulton. I have a deal for you. You're a gambling man. I been thinking about striking out on my own lately. I could use a good luck charm, too."

"Ain't you independent all of a sudden," said Forbes.

"But you owe me back wages from when I started four years ago," said the stranger.

"What's your deal? I'm not worried. I know you'll be running back here if you go out on your own and lose your ass."

"Let's play for it. I'll tell you what, my back wages against the girl: if Winifred can guess my name in three tries, she goes with me. If she can't guess it, she goes with you and you don't have to pay me."

Fulton Forbes filled his brandy snifter, took his Big Hunk out of it and fellatiated it nastily, and said, "Sure boy. I'll give you a fighting chance." He turned to her. "Go ahead little lady. Try to guess his name." Then he cackled hideously.

Winifred looked from one man to the other, and then realized the stranger must have some trick for letting her know just what his name was. She stared at him a long while, studying his fine strands of hair, then followed his gaze when he looked away as though that would give away the secret. She then panicked and wondered if he was signalling by blinking in code.

She realized she'd have to start. She looked at the wall. "Is it Bernard?" she asked. Forbes had a picture of a St. Bernard on the wall along with a few prints of setters and pointers hunting birds in fields.

"No, it sure ain't," chortled Forbes.

Winifred went rigid. The look on the stranger's face was enigmatic, if not simply blank. He must have been signalling somehow, but she still couldn't see his tricks.

"Is it Trevor?" The name popped into her mind for no reason. She felt the sweat dripping down the sides of her body, and was aware of the smell of leather. She consciously tried to loosen her tight stomach muscles.

"It ain't that neither," said Fulton a little too quickly. He was blushing in anticipation.

"Look," Winnie said, "I don't think this is fair. No one asked *me*." She was stalling for time, in one last desperate attempt to communicate, to understand the language the stranger was flashing his signals in.

"Too bad girl," Forbes stared cruelly at her and stirred his brandy with his Big Hunk. "You don't have anything to say about it. Guess again. It's your last try."

The stranger sat quietly, looking extremely attractive. He didn't appear to be concerned one way or the other.

She sighed. All was lost. "Is it . . . Robert?" she asked in a somewhat more high-pitched tone of voice.

"Ha ha!" shouted Forbes. "I won!"

The stranger moved fast. He pulled out a derringer from his vest pocket and aimed it at Forbes' heart.

Forbes' glee turned to befuddlement.

"Into the closet," the stranger ordered him.

"What're you doing?" The rancher couldn't quite grasp the turnaround. "You can't do this!" he cried. "What do you think you're doing?"

"I'm cheating," said the stranger. He pushed Forbes into the closet and turned the key in the lock, leaving it there. "The cook will let you out later."

Then he took Winifred by the arm and said, "Let's go."

Their getaway would have been assured, but suddenly in the living room, just as they were trying to run out the front door, the stranger started to shake and moan. He slumped against the wall and sweat poured off his forehead and upper lip.

Winnie ran over to him, as he leaned against the wall, his arms crossed in front of him, clutching himself. He was gritting his teeth and clenching his jaw, and he trembled all over.

"What's wrong?" she cried, thinking it was some kind of epileptic seizure.

"Identity Crisis!" he gasped. "All that playing in there," he looked back towards the game room.

"What?"

"All that business about my name. I hoped it wouldn't get to me, but I was wrong. You don't know what it's like to have such a silly name. No one ever uses it. I never get called anything by anyone. Do you know how that feels after a while? Sometimes I look in the mirror and I don't even know it's me. I'm like a nothing, not there in reality, I don't really exist. Sometimes I don't even know who I am!"

"Well, what is your name?"

"Don't laugh. Rumpelstiltskin." He seemed to relax a little.

Winnie could hear Forbes yelling from the closet. If they didn't move soon, some of his hired help would catch them. She said, "It's a wonderful name. But if we don't get going, Fulton's ranch hands are going to carve it into your head."

30

Rumpelstiltskin rallied. "You're right," he said. He ran over to the front door and threw it open, turning back to smile at her. The station wagon was there in front of the house, but they didn't want the police after them for grand theft. They ran behind the bunkhouse to the left of the main house where Rumpelstiltskin had his pickup parked. Strangely, no one chased after them: even though Forbes wasn't a popular man, any one of his ranch hands would have engaged in a high speed chase, just for the fun of it.

Winnie's problems were not over, though. Once they were safely away from the Double F land, driving along the highway at eighty miles an hour, Rumpelstiltskin began to talk. He went on and on, as though to make up for lost time.

"When I was old enough to realize I was different from everyone else," he began, holding the steering wheel lightly, "I had to wonder why my parents named me what they did. Cruelty? Misplaced assertion of individuality? After a long lost relative? They were very religious Baptists, you know, my family, and just before I was born . . ."

Winnie liked him enough to endure the autobiography, getting through it by way of sexual fantasies with him later that night in some motel room. There was nothing really wrong with him but his name, and privately she resolved to call him "Slim" from then on.

LITTLE RED RIDING HOOD

Real Theme: Dread

Little Red Riding Hood was not, as was formerly believed, a Communist. Not even a Socialist. Not even a Liberal. She had no politics. She believed political activism was passé, a nineteenth century eccentricity, something suitable for the idle and the inept. Also, contrary to another analysis by a leading thinker, neither was she wearing red to express a passionate nature, nor to evoke one. Her grandmother had given her the riding hood to wear, to keep her hair from flying around while sporting about in the back seat of her parents' new Rambler when the family took trips through backwoods Mississippi, the true location of this story. It just so happened that Granny chose red. Actually Little Red Riding Hood didn't like it that much and hardly ever wore it, so when Red's mother told her to take the basket of cakes and oatmeal cookies to Granny's house, she also instructed the girl to wear the coat to show Granny it was being used.

Red's mother's name was Large Blue Muumuu, after the housedress she always wore. Blue had over two hundred pounds of flesh, and it may be safely assumed that she ingested her share of the cakes and cookies. Granny was a trimmer and altogether neater person; her name was Pale Yellow Apron.

Red had a very common contemporary problem that is concertedly apolitical. She had Dread, a form of angst that leaves the heart palpitating and the hands clenched. The existential form of it is derived from the Isaac-Abraham story: what happens to the poor kid put through a trauma like that? Red felt her Dread physically, the palpitating of her heart, clenched hands, sweat, and the shakes, and the only thing she could do to get over an attack was to try to get involved in some activity that distracted her mind. But Dread is very hard to escape; it, as do all the other forms of angst, makes life not worth living. The victim knows something terrible is going to happen, but doesn't know what it is or exactly when it's going to happen. Since assuredly *something* terrible is going to happen *sometime*, Dreaders are right. But their cognition of it is worse than the actual thing happening because it disables them from enjoying the present moment. They are always worried about the disaster (storm, earthquake, disease, war, black hole, whatever), sure to hit sometime—any minute now.

Thus, Red, though not paranoid, was in Dread as she paced nervously through the forest with Blue's basket over her arm, garbed in Yellow's red Riding Hood. Her Dread could have conjured the wolf as a phantom in the woods, which, since she expected it with such certainty, appeared as the long-awaited disaster. But there is ample evidence on file at the county sheriff's office that she did encounter the wolf on her way to Granny's and did tell him the way to get there in the false trust created by her embarrassment over the fear she felt. Why the wolf didn't simply accost her there in the forest, take the basket, or eat Red if that was his intention, which still seems unclear, is a mystery which may never be solved. It would have been safer to eat her there than to eat her in Granny's house where paw

33

prints and identifying fur could be found. There is a great deal of darkness and controversy over the wolf, and since he was put out of commission permanently, it is a question whether he was a pathological child molester or just a small-time thief with the intention of establishing his own frightening but unmistakeable modus operandi in his crimes.

Red, then, reached Granny's just in time to find the wolf in bed in Granny's nightclothes. Everyone seems to compulsively point out the use of beds in fairy tales, as some matter of crucial significance, though there is ample justification for such furniture in these stories. Another more subtle aspect of the wolf's behavior is the role reversal here: was the performance in Granny's nightgown really just the playing out of a long repressed homosexual fantasy? Was the wolf some kind of monster or only a slightly disturbed victim of society's strict codes of conformity?

Red, to return to the facts, approached the bedside, having immediately recognized the wolf as the same one that she had given an oatmeal cookie to on the trail through the forest. She gave him a scornful look for being so obvious in his disguise, and then she decided the best course of action was to pretend she was fooled. Besides, she knew if she ran he would only chase her and eat her or maybe worse. When the disaster finally hits, Dreaders are usually calm, often relieved.

"What big eyes you have," she said. She tried not to look around to find out where Yellow was (maybe just her partially devoured corpse), so as not to give away to the wolf that she was onto his game.

The wolf did his bit.

"And, Grandmother, what big ears you have."

And so on. Predictably.

Red, by this time, was beginning to feel, not just disgusted, but downright angry at the wolf and his attempts at intimidation. In the very clutches of being devoured, she realized that

34

Dread had made her life hellish. This sleazy worm of a wolf didn't deserve the dignity of being feared. She looked straight at those gruesome fangs and said:

"And what decayed teeth you have, you woman-devouring, scum-carrying, son-of-a-bitch. Too goddamned cowardly to eat men, you have to pick on old ladies and little girls, you perverted transvestite misfit of society. If it weren't for you and your terrorist tactics the world might be a worthwhile place to live."

This is the quote that got Red in so much trouble with the Birch Society. Conservative reviews and quarterlies jumped on the exhortation as a clear example of Communist Ideology. While she really needs no defense for expressing herself honestly, it is vital to keep the record straight, and there is validity in the suggestion that Red, being of a somewhat poetic nature, was simply grasping onto the contemporary idiom to use an easily available metaphoric structure to make her noteworthy and vehement statement of rage. There is ample evidence in the case of Little Red Riding Hood that, because Large Blue Muumuu had brought her up alone, (since her husband, Pocketless Leather Vest, had left them long ago to join the merchant marine), and Blue herself having been raised by the widowed Pale Yellow Apron, Red had an understandable fear, if not dread, of the male sex. The wolf as a symbol of this, and her fury and casting of the blame for *all* her dread, which was not *all* male-caused, upon him, proves a purging theory, which is the most justifiable one because after this event Red lost her fears and anxieties, went on to college, was, during the Vietnam War, lightly involved with some mild protest groups and demonstrations, and subsequently married a stockbroker and now has two daughters. She has admitted, with some glee, that recurrences of that early dread are nonexistent, and she is now quite happy and well-adjusted, with her only problem being a somewhat predictable tendency to gain weight. This may be attributable to the fact that she loves to cook. Anyway, there is no need to proffer a moral where a celebration is applicable.

Back to the occasion in question, where several more issues need to be taken up for all the information available to be brought to light. Needless to say, the cakes and cookies came in handy as refreshments for the investigating officers, ambulance drivers, and men from the coroner's office. One facet that was long-discussed by all parties involved was the question of the severity and brutality of the woodcutter's deed. To kill the wolf may have been a terrible misuse of justice. It was later discovered, by testimony at the inquest by the wolf's entire family, his parole officer (for the wolf had been up on check-bouncing charges twice before), and several character witnesses, that the wolf was a strict vegetarian, and in fact was brought to extreme nausea by the thought of flesh, any flesh, even more so by human flesh. It may be that he was on a lark just to steal the goodies in the basket, thus turning the woodcutter's violent and barbarous murder into an abomination, if not a crime itself. However, self-defense would probably convince a jury, most of which are notoriously anti-wolf these days, and if that's not enough, it doesn't matter because no one is pressing charges against him since the woodcutter is very popular in the district. Suffice it to say that the wolf was surely reprehensible for his behavior, but capital punishment may have been an excessively severe sentence.

Granny, as all know, was locked in the bathroom during the Red-wolf encounter, after having been chased all around the room by the wolf. She was armed with a skillet that had probably been out on the stove or countertop, and with which she had landed one blow on the wolf's skull, a fact substantiated by the autopsy, and by the blood that was found on the pillowcase, which was the same type as that of the wolf. Why did she not call out to Red to warn her about the wolf? Some say she tried, but the acoustics of the bathroom were so good sound was muffled if the door was closed. It is possible that she had already seen the woodcutter passing and had by then crawled out the little window to bring him to aid the situation, herself in a nightgown and nearly too weak to climb to the high window after having wrestled with the flu for two weeks.

Now, to the question of the woodcutter. Some have viewed him as a reduction symbol, who, by the act of chopping down trees, was in this way an inspiration to Red and so partly, if not wholly, responsible for the ending of the wilderness of Dread in Little Red Riding Hood. Large Blue Muumuu herself brought up this possibility, glad that her daughter no longer had the sweaty fits of anxiety and nerves. Other critics have questioned the deus ex machina appearance of the woodcutter in exactly the right place at exactly the right moment. Still others have placed him as the dramatic foil, in direct opposition to the wolf (he was a strikingly handsome man), and this school of thought is the one that hinted at a certain Electra complex between Red and the woodcutter. In a free society maximum freedom and widest variance of opinion possible should be cultivated, so there's no reason to discredit any of these theories.

The true facts of the matter are that the woodcutter, at the time some thirty-five years of age and a good voting Democrat, though not a member of the woodcutters' union, which then didn't have a closed shop, was passing through the forest on his way to a woman's house. He had been involved with this woman, who, because she was married to someone else, implored the press to keep her name out of print, and the path to her house went right by Pale Yellow Apron's house, so there was no real wonder at his timely but random appearance. He had not previously been acquainted with Red or her family, and after the wolf incident had been cleared up, he never again had social contact with any of them.

CINDERELLA

Real Theme: Mediocrity

The focal point, and the most neglected, of the Cinderella story was not the fact that in the end the glass slipper she had lost trying to escape the ball before midnight fit her and not the sisters; but was instead the brouhaha aroused by that event between the two sisters. Before the incident they had gotten along perfectly, supportive and loving, but after both trying and failing to put their size 9's into petite Cindy's size 4 slipper, the two experienced a breach that was never smoothed over. Cindy, having left with Brian (the young man), as we all know lived happily, if not ever after, then at least for the majority of the time. She never saw the sisters after the elopement and never knew of their split; that may explain why most experts miss the point of this fairy tale: inter-feminine rivalry.

Contrary to the abridged versions, which depict her as at least *potentially* beautiful, Cindy was not a typically beautiful fairy tale character. She had a small mouth with thin lips, and her nose was a small acute triangle above the mouth. Her eyes had sparse lashes and brows and were gently slanted in an intriguing but not quite oriental way. She was not beautiful by any means and never would be, but she had an infectious attractiveness, and her sincere and concerned manner made her company desirable to everyone once she was out from under the rotten step-family.

Cindy's father had been a cello player in the Boston Symphony and Cindy was devoted to him. She never knew her mother, who had died of accidental food poisoning from eating a can of diet fruit cocktail that was no good. This had happened just after Cindy was born when the mother was trying to lose the weight she had gained during pregnancy. So Cindy's father brought her up, and though they had been a bit lonely, they were, nonetheless, happy. At the age of ten, this all changed for Cindy. Her father married the cruel and deceitful Chloe, not knowing her true personality, and into the family came the three harpies who made Cindy's life so miserable after her father died of a premature heart attack four years later, which had probably been brought on by the nagging and demanding selfishness of the stepmother and two stepsisters. It was no time before Leonora and Linda, both blondes who, several years older than Cindy, already wore bright lipstick and eye makeup, made their little stepsister into their personal slave. They forced her to do their chores around the house, saying they would tell their mother that Cindy was fooling around with Richard, the young man next door. Knowing the stepmother could never believe her, Cindy wisely submitted to the evil sisters' demands. The stepmother gave the sisters her department store charge plates so they could buy any clothes they wanted, but she made Cindy wear the old worn-outs and hand-me-downs. Every way possible the three conspired to oppress and tyrannize Cindy.

Cindy was dreadfully unhappy in these years. They had moved to Brooklyn. She did as she had to, but she kept quiet and to herself as much as possible. Every night before she fell asleep, she had a pretend conversation with her father, telling him the situation and assuring him that she would last until she was eighteen and could legally move out. Sometimes she dreamed that he came back and took her away to a beautiful house in the country where they listened to classical music and were happy again. But in reality Cindy had no friends and no family, no one at all to talk to, and she was resigned to being alone until she could get out on her own.

One day she was waxing Chloe's Chevrolet station wagon. Leonora and Linda were out shopping for new dresses to wear to the sock hop to be held at the high school gymnasium that night. Cindy, as usual, was not to be included: they never suspected she would even want to go, being such a square, because the music would be played by a rock band. So Cindy set to work that afternoon, a little disappointed and wishing there would be someone, anyone, who meant something to her.

After finishing the car, she sat in the parking space against the post that held up the roof and peeled dried crusty wax from her fingers. That was when Dave showed up. Dave was her fairy godfather. The traditional story had Cinderella being helped by a fairy godmother, but recent discoveries have proven that the gender was changed to give the reader a more rounded view of womankind, the original author having felt that the facts couldn't stand for themselves but had to be manipulated to counterbalance the cruelty and nastiness of the stepsisters and stepmother.

Dave appeared to Cindy out of nowhere in a manner to be explained by parapsychologists and students of psychic phenomena, not by science, unless it really is true that matter may spontaneously, at the will of certain highly integrated and powerful minds, change from energy into substance and back again. But even if this were possible, would we be able to use the power responsibly? Aside from the moral questions, it must be admitted that Dave indeed simply condensed out of the air like a raindrop, with a sparkling of light, which was probably energy given off in a chemical reaction similar to what happens when clouds condense into rain, and with a flourish of chimes the presence of which is completely unexplainable.

Dave dusted a few sparkles of light from his arms and legs. He turned to Cinderella and said, "Why so glum? You ought to be excited about the sock hop tonight."

"I'm not going," answered Cindy, looking at him with much suspicion. Then she became curious: "How did you do that sparkling light and chimes thing, anyway?"

"Oh easy. All fairy godparents travel that way."

"Fairy godparent?"

"Sure. We're around most of the time, and unless something goes terribly wrong, we help our adopted human children get through the difficulties of life." Dave wore brown slacks and a gray sweatshirt and was about forty-five, still in fairly good shape but tired-looking.

"I thought Disneyland was just for kids."

"Well, the media only likes to bring you the positive side of what fairy godparents do. So often there are problems in fairyland like those on earth: drugs, violence, neglect of duty, and too many people never get to meet or be helped by their designated guardian. All problems can't be corrected, but that shouldn't disillusion everyone completely."

"Oh," said Cindy.

"Now, what do you mean, you're not going to the dance?"

She shrugged. "I'm not going. That's all. Besides the fact that my family won't let me, I don't have a dress to wear and I have no ride, so I really don't want to go. Think of it: all those people packed into one room, all of them pretty much the same, all equally banal, listening to mediocre egalitarian music that

41

any of them could perform equally well. I seek higher forms of stimulation."

"Hmmm," said Dave, distressed for a moment. "I guess that's one thing I'm not able to solve for you. Mediocrity is the price of democracy, and banality is the result of mediocrity. At least we have our freedom."

Cindy just looked at him.

"Anyway, so what? Look, do your sisters or your stepmother have an old dress you can wear?"

"I'm too small to fit their things."

Dave sighed patiently. "I know a great alterations woman in the Bronx. She'll whip it out this afternoon if I enchant her a bit. Don't worry about a thing."

"But how will I get there?"

Dave laughed. "How little faith you have. You stop your whining and let me arrange all that. I'll bring you the dress in a couple of hours. Meanwhile, take a bath, wash and set your hair, and try to get yourself in a more cheerful frame of mind."

Cindy said, "O.K." and followed instructions as she always did.

True to his word, Dave returned about six after the sisters had locked themselves in the bathroom. They were giggling and screaming things about hairspray and deodorant. Chloe was in her private bathroom off the master bedroom, and she was getting ready for her own date. Cindy was unobserved in the kitchen washing up the dinner dishes when Dave appeared in the doorway and startled her.

"Psssst!" he said.

"What? Oh, it's you," she said as she quickly turned.

"Look at this," he said, proudly. He held the dress she had filched from Chloe's closet. It was on a hanger. "It's just your size now."

Cindy's hair was up in a bandana, to hide the curlers. "It does look pretty," she admitted. She wiped her hands on her apron, then handled the dress and checked the seams. "What about the rest? I'll need shoes, a purse, a coat. And not to seem repetitious, but how will I get there and back?"

"I saved the best for last." From behind his back, Dave produced a small evening bag, a short silk coat, and the exquisite clear glass slippers.

This finally got to Cindy. "Oh they're beautiful!" she gasped.

"Now I'm happy," said Dave. "I finally made you excited. Now, after the others have gone, get yourself dressed and go out in front." He smiled. "I've arranged for your date . . ."

" . . . my date?"

"Don't worry. He's a wonderful young man, Brian Harris. He'll pick you up. Look for a red TR-4."

"I hope he's not the same as all the other boys I know."

"Well, kid, even if he is, why don't you just try to enjoy it and not worry about whether it's banal or mediocre. You'll have to have some fun sometime in your life."

"O.K." Cinderella said.

"Now, the only drawback is, you've got to get back before midnight, so the sisters and mother won't know you were out. They'll all turn into monsters if they know you're having a good time."

"Won't they recognize me at the dance?"

"Not a chance. Here, this dust will make you so beautiful no one will be able to look at you long enough to recognize you." He sprinkled a bit of some radioactive dust on her. "Don't worry: it won't hurt you in small quantities. It'll make you have a good time."

Cindy did as she was told. She waited until ther others were gone, then got dressed, did her hair, tried on a bit of rouge and lipstick, and went downstairs to wait in front for this Brian Harris character in his red TR-4. He arrived after a couple of minutes, leaning over the passenger's seat to open the door of the roofless car.

"You Cinderella?"

"Yes," she said, and got daintily into the car.

He said no more, but drove at an extremely fast rate to the high school gymnasium. Cindy had to put her hands over her hair to keep it from getting messed up. She had only looked at him once when she got into the car, but it was enough to notice that he was typical for a boy his age: casually groomed with a look of self-assurance mixed with abandon.

They arrived at the dance and checked their coats and shoes at the door. They said little and danced a lot. She looked around at all the people in the gym. Sameness, sameness. She was the same, too, except for the glass slippers which, ironically, she was not able to wear. But every time she sat down and started to mope, along came Brian to ask her to dance. She began to like him, common as he was.

Then it got on to midnight and they had to go. She had seen her stepsisters once or twice, but they hadn't recognized her. Then Linda appeared right next to her at the coat check. The boy behind the counter had only found one glass slipper and was searching for the other. Cindy, losing faith in the magic dust, rushed out, Brian following closely, before the other shoe had been located, so Linda would not accidentally discover her.

Brian dropped her off, and without even a kiss goodnight, he called after her, "Can I see you again?"

"I don't care," she called back, running up the stairs in her nylons, holding the one glass slipper.

Well, the rest is a matter of record. Thinking it would be a good excuse to call on her the next day, Brian went back and got the other glass slipper. When Chloe opened the door and saw him standing there in front of his TR-4 looking for the owner of the shoe, she immediately called her two daughters down, thinking he had money. Their comments to each other regarding foot size need not be repeated.

Cindy saw Brian and decided this was her chance. She packed her suitcase and sneaked out the back door and down the block. She flagged him down once he left the house. They ran away to St. Louis, where he had a sympathetic aunt who put them up for a while until they were able to get jobs and find a place of their own. Cindy had to lie about her age, but no one asked for a birth certificate at the wedding, so everything was fine.

Dave, unfortunately, never found out what became of his human charge. Upon non-materializing back into his own realm, he nearly knocked over Rapunzel's fairy godmother, Debbie, staggering down the street under the influence of radioactive dust, which she did not use in moderation, but was addicted to. Dave spent the rest of eternity trying to reform her, or at least protect her from hurting herself or anyone else.

SLEEPING BEAUTY

Real Theme: Ennui

We all believed that Sleeping Beauty, the mythical name of a real person named Thorn Rose, sometimes nicknamed Briar, was under enchantment, the victim of an evil spell cast by the thirteenth wise woman in the kingdom. Since there had been only enough place settings for twelve, only twelve wise women had been invited, and the thirteenth took the social snub personally, although it had not been so intended. The first eleven wise women were supposed, according to early versions, to have given Thorn the qualities of beauty, virtue, riches, all the usual, and when the angry and neglected thirteenth wise woman arrived, she rudely interrupted the gift giving to inform everyone that her own gift was that the baby would prick her finger in her fifteenth year and die. Fortunately, the twelfth wise woman was still available to give a gift, so she moderated the curse so that Thorn and everyone else would only fall asleep for a hundred years. Then a handsome prince would kiss her, wake her and the rest of the kingdom, and they would all predictably live happily ever after.

46

On deeper investigation, it has been discovered that all this is, in fact, simply not true. Thorn's father, to set the record straight, was not a king but the proprietor of a small vacuum cleaner repair shop in New York City. Her mother was a seamstress who specialized in irregular alterations. (It was Mrs. Rose, in fact, who altered Cinderella's gown.) Thorn's father was the son of Polish immigrants and was accustomed to, not royal splendor and prosperity, but extreme poverty. After many years of hard work in a sardine factory, he saved enough to open his own business, having learned appliance repair at night school, and after accepting repairs at home to do in his spare time, to pad his savings.

He had been open five years before he felt established enough to marry. Betsy Thorn, the former Betsy Baker, was a pretty young woman, the youngest daughter in a family of twelve girls. Rose courted her briefly and married her, expecting to start his own family, hopefully starting with a boy, but, alas, time passed and Betsy did not get pregnant. They tried everything. No luck. Finally they went to a doctor. Rose's sperm count was O.K. (He already knew this, having impregnated a girl from the sardine factory when he was nineteen, a situation he was forced to handle with an abortion, not only because of the poverty he was in at the time, but because of the girl, who did not fit into his future plans, and who later became a professional, since the doctor had inadvertently sterilized her during the abortion. (He did not want Betsy to know about this though, so he pretended he didn't know about his sperm count)). The doctor who tested them discovered that Betsy had collapsed ovaries.

A couple of sad years went by. Right about the time they were getting ready to adopt, there was a sign (and this part is similar to the traditional story); Rose discovered a dead frog that had been run over by a vacuum-cleaner-bag delivery van in front of his shop. On the flattened back of the frog body were printed the words, "You will have a beautiful daughter." Sure enough, Betsy missed her period that month and when she went back to her doctor to take the pregnancy test, sure enough the rabbit died. The doctor told her it was a miracle, the ovaries had mysteriously inflated to their normal size and had begun ovulating normally. "Modern science cannot yet explain every phenomenon," said the doctor apologetically.

The Roses were ecstatic, and spent the remainder of the pregnancy visiting their friends and families to exult over the exciting and long-desired event. The baby was born after a harrowing ride to the hospital in Rose's pickup, and the christening was planned a month later. It was Betsy's mother and eleven sisters who gave all the nice presents and wished all the best things in life: beauty, a car on her sixteenth birthday, good grades, a rich husband, etc. The sisters went first, each presenting a check or clothes and furniture for the present time. Then, as they were all fondling the incredibly beautiful and well-mannered baby, there was a knock at the door. Rose answered it. To his astonishment, it was the woman he had previously gotten pregnant. She had carried a torch for him ever since, besides having been deeply insulted by his unwillingness to marry her, and blamed him for her subsequent turn to the streets for a living. She pushed aside one sister who was leaning over the smiling and gurgling baby saying "Awhh, how cute," and silence fell over the room. Here stood a horrible woman in a black sequinned evening dress, smoking a cigarette and glaring with hurt disgust from Rose to the baby. She blew smoke in the baby's face, causing Thorn to cough and cry.

"Oh, you're beautiful all right," she said to the baby while sneering at the others, "and you'll be good and kind, and vote, maybe even serve on a jury. And you'll go to CCNY and meet an accountant and move to the suburbs to have your own little insignificant family. But one thing you'll never have, and this I'll guarantee: you'll never have any brains."

Then the abomination, smelling of Midnight Rendezvous perfume, left with a self-righteous flounce and a wicked smile under all her makeup.

Betsy's mother broke the icy, shocked silence that followed, by saying, "How silly. As pretty as she is, I'm sure she'll grow up to marry a brain. Maybe a professor at Columbia." It wasn't long before tempers and feelings had been placated and everyone forgot all about it.

Later that night, after everyone else had gone, Rose told Betsy about the affair he had had so long ago with the evil woman and they chalked it up to envy and bad taste. They never saw the loathsome curser again because several days later she was arrested and imprisoned. She extended her sentence by joining in a prison riot that failed to improve conditions, and then was shortly thereafter stabbed to death by a black woman inmate whom she had called "Bitch."

Well, the years went by and Thorn became phenomenally beautiful. Everyone commented on it. Betsy's greatest pleasure was to take Thorn shopping with her so all the other women could fawn and dote on her. At six years the girl was so poised and graceful that her mother enrolled her in ballet school. Thorn was virtuous and kind as well as beautiful and talented, earning more Brownie merit badges and awards than anyone in history. Betsy sewed all the child's clothes, so she was always well-dressed, which merely accentuated Thorn's beautiful features and bearing.

About the time Thorn was in her sophomore year in high school, however, she was terribly bored with the whole thing. She was sick and tired of being whistled at, being told she was gorgeous, and being popular. Thorn's mother tried to talk to her about her apparent unhappiness, but the miserable teenager was unapproachable until one day in April. It was beautiful and springlike outside, and Thorn came home in tears and threw herself down on the bed.

"Thorn, darling," said Betsy, holding her around the shoulders. "Whatever is the trouble?"

"It's just that I'm so stupid," she sobbed. "I hate it. I don't even need to be smart because I'm so beautiful and charming that a brain would only spoil my attractiveness and lessen my power. But yech! It's such a drag!"

Betsy looked at her daughter in terror, and immediately went downstairs and reported the incident to Rose. Neither of them mentioned the curse given at the christening party but it was on both their minds. Remembering every detail of the moment vividly, they both hurried upstairs.

"Princess, Princess," said Rose, "Tell Daddy what the trouble is. Whatever you want, Daddy will get it for you, and whatever is wrong Daddy will fix it up for his little princess."

She turned to him in fury, with her tear-filled eyes wide open. "So," she said, "You'll do everything. All I have to do is sit here and look good. Is that life?" She practically lunged at him, but her mother held her back as Thorn shouted, "And take that milk toast sweet talk and shove it! It makes me want to throw up!"

It turned out that Thorn had been embarrassed by the English class intellectuals, who made her feel worthless because she was unable to textually defend a comment she made about a Hemingway novel: that Frederick and Katherine never really loved each other.

From then on, her only desire in life was to become an intellectual, a situation made impossible by her dazzling beauty, deep blue eyes that could corrupt the most puritanical teacher, dark brown hair seductively curled at the shoulder, and her rather fully developed bust. Any personal contact with intelligent people was impossible. The minute she walked into a room all attention was on her in a quite obvious sensual, not intellectual, way.

She tried cloistering herself to read all the important works of the human intelligence on her own, to teach herself and develop her own mind, but reading always made her go to sleep.

So Thorn was cast into an irremediable and seemingly permanent state of *ennui*. Whatever her beauty, charm, virtue, and other talents could get her, she didn't want. What a waste were all those low-minded activities such as modelling, secretary, housewife, mother, and the rest of the possibilities she could conceive as being in her future. She would stand near a doorway, watching her mother industriously sewing at her machine, and Thorn would dream of having herself killed by hiring a tatooist to cover her body with obscene words. She didn't want to go on. Her opportunities were too limiting. There was no reason to be awake; she might as well sleep through eternity, letting people love her and emulate her.

This went on, not for a hundred years, but for eight years, until Thorn was 23. At that time she had taken to the habit of lonely wanderings about the city, taking buses through the slums and downtown, climbing to the tops of skyscrapers for panoramas. She decided to go to the Statue of Liberty. It seemed like a good joke—ironic in the extreme. Besides, she had never been there, so she might as well go; it was probably going to be a bore, but so what? So was not going.

She took the boat ride out, walked to the top, came back. Stepping off the boat she had her first glimpse, not of the handsome prince, but of a young man whose ugliness complemented her own beauty. He was shorter than she was, and bony, balding prematurely, and his skin was sallow and white. He wore dirty jeans and a drab shirt half tucked in. His plastic frame glasses were twenty years out of date. She first spied him walking into an alley, and when she followed him curiously, she found him writing "entropy" on the wall of a building with a can of dayglo spray paint.

51

"Wow," she thought, recognizing the word from an article in the *New York Review of Books*, which she read cover to cover to improve her mind. "What a brilliant person he must be!" She fell in love with him immediately.

He really never gave her a glance, but she began following him and trying to talk to him; she somehow needed to find out if he knew anyone at Columbia. He told her she was too stupid to get in, so there was no use trying.

For weeks she pestered him, forcing herself on him even though he did nothing to encourage her and even insulted her brutally. When he called her bird-brain, she loved it. She said, "Yes, my brain is soaring with ideas. Thanks to you I'm learning to think. I can even read Dostoevsky without falling asleep!"

He would stay up all night with his friends arguing Eternal Recurrence, or aesthetics, or linguistic patterns in poetry, and soon Thorn was joining in the conversations, if only to ask a question and get the name of an author or a book to read next.

Finally he began to realize he would not be able to get rid of her. He sat down one morning, when the sun was rising, after an all night discussion, and gave her his terms of acceptance. "Look, why don't you wear jeans and tie your hair back. You look like you're posing for the cover of *Vogue* all the time. You should swear a little more and make assertions instead of asking questions. And get rid of that stupid smile and look real for a change. What do you think life is, a big party?"

She followed his instructions gladly, which annoyed him, but it was better than looking superficial. She practiced being real, alternately starving herself and overeating. She got bags under her eyes from the sleepless nights spent worrying about the destiny of mankind. So he hadn't remade her in his own image, but merely freed her from the results of all the gifts her family had given her all her life.

They decided not to get married because the divorce rate was so high the odds were stacked against them. They decided not to have children since the world was full of children already and there were too few responsible adults. They moved to Philadelphia and lived hand to mouth with few possessions.

So Sleeping Beauty and the intellectual did not live happily ever after. They are still together, though, even through the hardships of modern urban life. Thorn visits her parents infrequently. They are both silently relieved the prophesy about her hadn't come true, but compared to the amount of suffering she was putting herself through, it's not much consolation.

THE SHOEMAKER
AND THE ELVES

Real Theme: Schizophrenia

This story was an early attempt to explain the psychological phenomenon of schizophrenia. Because of the early prejudices against the science, the public had to be informed of the malady by way of watered-down metaphors. Now that we in the twentieth century are grown up, we can cope with this problem in an open and honest way.

The shoemaker's wife had read an article about schizophrenia in the *Reader's Digest*, and she quickly identified it as the problem her husband had. "I should have known it would happen sooner or later," she told herself, lugging a green plastic basket full of wet laundry out to the back yard to hang up on the clothesline. Her name was Hilda and she was fifty-four years old. All her hair was gray, but she curled it every day, and she kept the rest of her appearance up with makeup, exercise, and plenty of sleep. Age was no different to her than youth; now she just had a little more experience.

Her husband, Henry Wilson, was sixty. For him turning sixty was a critical blow. Forty wasn't bad, and at fifty he could still say, "Oh, I'm not old yet, not really," but at sixty there was no denying it. He was old. His face had taken on the quality of the leather he had worked every day for forty-five years, his hands were laced with veins, and his hair was nearly gone except for a few racy streaks combed behind his ears, that could have been painted on with silver paint. He used to think his eyes sparkled and his smile was responsible for the good business he had enjoyed in the past. Now he felt that absence of cheerfulness, due to age, had likewise *hurt* his business.

Things had gone badly all year. Three days before he had hobbled over to his shop on his two tired legs and looked through all his cupboards to find almost nothing in them to justify the exercise. In one there were three empty packing boxes and in another a couple of broken tools he had meant to have fixed. Only in the last cupboard, which he had avoided because it was low and because he'd have to bend over to look in it, did he find barely enough half-dried leather to make a pair of shoes. He oiled it up as nicely as possible so it could be worked with, and he cut out the sandal pattern that he'd found in his newest catalogue.

Then he walked the eight blocks back to the house. Boise had built up so much in the years he'd been there that it was hard to remember how it had been when he first had the house built. 1925 it was, five years after he started the business. Times had been decent for him then, even with the depression, and since they had no children, for no reason he could think of, between the two of them there was enough in the savings account and in equity in the business to apply for a loan to build the house. It had been theirs for twenty-five years now. Idaho wasn't theirs anymore, though. Commercialism had seduced people away from handmade shoes. The last ten years had been such a struggle that the savings account had been emptied, loans on the house and business had been taken just to pay taxes and insurance and stay open, and now the car was going to have to be sold to pay for groceries.

The little wooden house was on a street of other little wooden houses that had all been there long enough to comfort him as he walked by. "Never mind," he said to himself, "I'll make that pair of shoes tomorrow and sell the car. Things will keep going for a little while." He walked in the front door of his house and said hello to Hilda. He took off his coat and sat in his easy chair in front of the television set.

"He looks a little strange," Hilda said to herself. "He looks so far away. I hope he's not sick. That would be the last straw."

She fixed dinner: soup made from some leftover meat and old vegetables that had been on sale at half price at the market. A kind neighbor had sent over a loaf of bread as well.

He thought, "God, I wish I had a smoke. A cigarette, a pipe, a cigar, even a chaw: anything." He'd had to give up tobacco at the beginning of their poor times several years ago. Hilda had nagged him that it was such a filthy habit and bad for his health, but he only gave it up when he couldn't afford it anymore. He sat and watched the news on TV. But he didn't pay attention to the stories being reported; he just watched the quirks and mannerisms of the newscasters and listened to the funny sounds of their voices. The film clips seemed to change independently of the stories.

Hilda brought him a bowl of soup and some bread. He ate it mechanically. She thought how he had resisted getting machines to do his work all these years. He insisted on making his shoes completely by hand, but it really hadn't helped him stay more human.

Henry ate and then changed the channel to comedy. He was tired. His hands were arthritic, his feet gouty, his heartburn fiercer, and his muscles and bones all tired. He fell asleep somewhere in the midst of prime time programming while Hilda was reading old copies of *Family Circle* she'd picked up dirt cheap at a garage sale. She woke him and put him to bed, then she went right to sleep herself.

In the morning Henry woke up feeling remarkably fresh. He dressed and then fixed some toast for breakfast. Without waking Hilda he almost danced to work, deciding that they could even subsist happily on Welfare if the business went under. When he opened the glass door of the shop, the bells over the door tinkled, and he saw on the workbench a completed pair of sandals. They were the most finely stitched and beautiful he'd ever seen. The stitches were so small and regular they must have been made with a special attachment on some new kind of machine. He looked closely at the leather. He identified the flaw that he knew had been on the leather he'd cut out the night before.

"My heavens!" he said to himself. He decided someone must have broken into the shop the night before and taken the leather off to a factory to make such fine sandals. It was hard to believe, but he could think of no other explanation.

However, before he got over his astonishment, a silver Jaguar XKE pulled up out front and a woman got out. She was well-dressed and had an air of luxury in the very way she walked and smiled. When she saw the sandals she said they were just the thing for her daughter, who was leaving for Europe this week. The woman gave Henry fifty dollars, asking if that was enough, and since he was stunned just by her presence, all he could do was nod. She smiled and took the sandals just as they were.

57

Henry wandered around the shop for a while, then called up the leather supply agents. He had no more credit, but they would allow him enough leather to make two pairs of shoes if he paid them the fifty dollars toward his account. He had wanted to buy some tobacco, but they demanded the entire fifty. He had to send a boy over to the warehouse to pick up the leather. The boy was eleven years old and rode a bicycle; he had been hanging around the shop for a year or two, helping Henry with cleaning up, and generally being company for the old man. Henry had given him some of the old tools in payment for errands because he'd been so hard up for money.

Henry had been thumbing through the catalogues as he waited for the leather. He had decided on another pair of sandals, in a different pattern, and a pair of nice boots. He only had time to cut out the leather during the afternoon because there were so many calls from bill collectors, it being the first of the month. He left the shop at six and walked home. Hilda had dinner ready, more soup and bread, and while they ate he told her about the sandals that had been finished before he got there and how he didn't know how they had been stitched so finely. She let him go on about how amazing it was; she figured he'd made them himself—he had been an intricate stitcher when his fingers were more supple. Why he should want to make up a story about not having done it or a story about someone else having done it was beyond her.

Then, the next day when he got to the shop and found the pair of sandals and the pair of boots on the workbench, completely sewn in the smallest, most even stitches he had ever seen, he was again amazed. He knew Hilda hadn't believed him, so he went right home and got her, brought her to the shop, and showed her the shoes. She began to think he really did have a nail loose somewhere. He'd had an uncle committed, and she began to fear Henry was showing signs of the family inclination to schizophrenia. Henry told her to look around the shop for evidence that someone else had done it and he assured her that it was impossible for him to sew such stitches anymore. Then he told her she would have to take his word that he had only cut out the leather the day before.

"I know she doesn't believe me," he said to himself.

"He's lost his mind," she said to herself.

Just then a young couple came into the shop. They explained that it was their first wedding anniversary and they wanted something special and personal to give to each other. Cost was no concern. They had seen the sandals and the boots through the window as they walked by. "Just the thing," said the tall young man. "They're just the right size, too. Will a hundred dollars be enough?"

"A hundred and ten," said Henry quickly, remembering the tobacco and the fact that the errand boy would soon have to be paid some cash if Henry expected him to keep fetching leather.

"Great," said the man. "Handmade shoes. It's a bargain whatever the price."

Hilda watched as the purchase was made and was not sure whether to let her mouth hang open in amazement or call for an ambulance. She did not say anything to herself, but decided to let Henry go on until he did something dangerous to himself or to someone else. So far it was simple delusions, and he was getting a lot of work done and finally making some money. Perhaps at his age he had to put himself in another mind just to get the shoes made. Later, though, when he insisted she stay there to watch him making the shoes, she thought perhaps there was something odd going on, and not Henry's mind going soft. Henry called the leather supply, arranged to pay a little more on his account, sent the boy over on his bicycle for the leather, and was able to pacify a few other creditors with small payments as well as save a little money to buy a pack of cigars.

Out of the new leather he cut patterns for four pairs of shoes, letting Hilda choose a couple of the latest styles from the catalogues. Then it was time to close up the shop and go home. Henry made sure Hilda noticed the exact location of the leather pieces, and he offered to handcuff himself to her for the night. She told him not to be ridiculous, but she did sleep so soundly that night that she couldn't have sworn that Henry didn't get up in the night to make the shoes. Anyway, first thing in the morning he dragged her down to the shop and with a portentous glint in his eye he unlocked the glass door and let Hilda walk in. He knew what she would find.

When she saw the shoes, Hilda said, without gasping or showing any agitation, "Henry, I think you'd better see a doctor."

"What for?" he said. "Look, something's going on here, and I have an idea how we can find out what it is. Let's hide in the back room tonight to wait for whoever or whatever does this for us, and get to the bottom of the mystery. I'll prove to you I'm telling the truth. Besides, we should thank them for saving our business, if not our very lives."

Reluctantly Hilda agreed, but she fell asleep, and the next morning when Henry told her it was two naked little elves who climbed in the ventilator duct and did the cobbling, she could only roll her eyes to heaven. He was feeling such gratitude for their work that he wanted to leave them each a set of clothes so they wouldn't have to be cold or risk being arrested for indecent exposure. Hilda thought this was taking the delusion a bit far, though she had to admit Henry was a new man, infused with new life. On the other hand, she felt that if his personality really was split, he should be getting some kind of professional attention, or at least that was what the article in *Reader's Digest* said. She couldn't remember all the details of the article (she had traded it for a *Woman's Day*), but she did remember something about the victim being unpredictable and capable of anything. Then she looked up the word *schizophrenic* in the dictionary on the bookshelf in the office, which took quite a while because of the way the word is spelled. The definition was general enough to include even herself at times.

"I'll just have to hope he's not dangerous and that this is a new beginning for us," she said to herself.

Of course, some people came in to buy the shoes that morning and with the money Henry bought more leather and took another step in climbing out of debt.

That afternoon, after he cut out the leather for the shoes, he made Hilda sit down and help him make the tiny outfits for the elves. From caps to shoes, the clothes were a *tour de force* of bad taste, since the shirts were red, the pants blue, the tunics green, and the caps purple. Henry said elves like clothes like that; they aren't color-coordinated like human beings.

Hilda rather enjoyed making the clothes, and she began to feel the exuberance Henry had been radiating. "Besides," she said to herself, as she was baking stuffed Cornish game hens and cooking asparagus tips in bearnaise sauce, "psychiatrists cost too much. And what could they do for Henry anyway? His uncle never got out once they locked him up. I'd rather have him this way than not at all."

Henry came home and chatted happily while he ate his dinner; then he returned to the shop. He laid the little suits of clothes next to the day's leather, and then he hid to wait for the elves. When they arrived, they put on their new clothes immediately and then began to dance around in delight. They took the pieces of cut-out leather, stitched up the new pairs of shoes, and left by climbing out the ventilator duct in the ceiling.

That was the last of the elves. Henry had to make his own shoes from then on out, but business got a lot better because handmade things had just become the fashion again, and he was able to make a lot of money so when he retired they didn't have to starve to death. Hilda never mentioned the aberration about the elves again and never asked what became of those little suits of strangely colored clothes. They both died within six months of each other, Henry of a heart attack and Hilda of a stroke, and they had spent all but a few thousand dollars which they had donated to charities as a provision in their wills. So there wasn't much left after them except all those shoes and no one who owned a pair really knew who had made them anyway, so it really didn't make much difference.

THE FISHERMAN AND HIS WIFE

Real Theme: Discontent

The fisherman was really a lobsterman named Tim Jarrett, who worked the coast of Maine, making quite a good living. He and his wife Joanne didn't live in a hovel, as we were told erroneously, but in a nice tri-level in Cape Elizabeth. Joanne didn't have to work, and she stayed at home every day, making big plans for their retirement and reading glamor magazines. Tim was content with things as they were, so he didn't want to think about the future. But he let her dream, thinking, "It's good for her. It keeps her busy."

Both of them had been advised by their doctor not to eat shellfish because of the cholesterol, which left no romance in Tim's job. He was ambitious but rather clumsy and inept, often dropping lobsters off the side of his boat by accident, and had he been more dextrous, or had he at least hired a more graceful and coordinated assistant, he might have been an extremely wealthy man.

63

His boat was paid for, though, and he felt like he had all a man could ask for. He was basically content and cheerful with his lot. In fact, he was so satisfied with his life that the day a lobster talked back to him he wasn't concerned a bit.

"Congratulations," said the somewhat small lobster, who was missing one claw.

"For what?" asked Tim.

"You've just caught me. I'm a magic lobster; really, I'm an enchanted prince caught in this lobster body by an evil witch. But for no sensible or understandable reason, the fact that you caught me entitles you to the free wish of your choice."

"Sure," said the skeptical and pragmatic Tim, packing his pipe with tobacco. Just like a mail advertising scheme, he thought.

"It's true," insisted the lobster. "I haven't been caught for hundreds of years, so I can do just about anything you can think of. My wish granting potential gets stored up if I don't use it, you see."

Tim tried to light his pipe, but the matches accidentally popped out of his hands and into the ocean. "So," he said, "do you get to go free or something after the wish?"

"Free?"

"I mean, will you turn back to your real self?"

"That depends on your definition of what is real," said the lobster, and then, after meditating a moment, "And what is a self." Then he waved his one claw resolutely, "But questions aside, make a wish and let's get on with it."

"I don't believe it," said Tim.

"You don't have to," returned the lobster haughtily.

"But I can't think of anything. I have my boat, my house, my wife. I'm happy."

The lobster sighed. "O.K. Just toss me back in, then. Someone else might catch me."

64

"Sure." Tim bent down to pick the lobster up off the deck of the boat and threw him back into the ocean. He quickly forgot the incident and went about his work, harvesting a good batch early in the day. When he got home and told Joanne about the strange encounter with the enchanted lobster, she was furious.

"You never think of anyone but yourself," she ranted. "You're happy. Of course you're happy. All you do is what you want twenty-four hours a day. Did you even think to consider me and what I want?"

"I consider you every day," Tim whined. "I have to get up at the crack of dawn and freeze half to death every morning catching something for other people to enjoy. And I used to love lobster, too. On the half shell. Drawn butter. Just a hint of lemon juice. Mmmm."

"You're so selfish! You never once thought that it might be hard for me to sit through all those long days with nothing to do."

Tim was shocked. "You could have done anything you wanted. You were free to come and go as you pleased. You always were. You are now."

"No I wasn't. I had to keep your home and prop up your ego when the fishing was bad. Did you ever think to buy me something nice in appreciation of my efforts? Like maybe a diamond, for example. Now get back out there and ask that lobster for a diamond; make it a big one, a pendant."

Tim said O.K. and took off for a sunset cruise. He called and called for the lobster, using the chants from every fairy tale he knew: "Mirror, mirror on the wall," "I'll huff and I'll puff . . .," "Who's been sleeping in my bed . . .?" Finally the lobster appeared off the bow of the boat.

"Can I still have that wish?" called Tim, not one to waste time with small talk.

"Yes," said the lobster. "What is it you want?"

"Well, I wouldn't do this just for myself, but my wife says she wants a diamond pendant. I think it's a bit excessive, but she insists that she needs something to make up for all those years of working for me and waiting for me. You know how women are."

"Go on home," said the lobster. "You've got your wish."

So there is was, a nine carat marquis-cut, dangling from the silk cord around her neck. Tim said to her, "Now you should be satisfied."

"I'll let you know in the morning," she replied with a prudent tone. She wore the pendant all night until they went to bed when she set it right next to her on the bedside table.

In the morning she woke him early, shaking him by the arm. "I dreamed I had a natural sable coat. I've always wanted one and I was always afraid to ask you for it. I'll bet you never once thought about getting me something like that. Go ask the lobster for a full-length natural sable coat."

"I can't do that," mumbled Tim, reaching for his glasses, but knocking them off the bedside table.

"Go," she commanded. "Siberian sable."

So he did, again invoking the lobster after a series of Mother Goose rhymes, and the lobster again said, "Go home. You got what you wanted."

Tim took Joanne out to dinner that night in Portland so she could show off her new treasures. She was in ecstasy the whole time and made quite a spectacle of herself in front of the other diners. But in the morning she was consumed again by discontent.

"Look," she said to Tim, over toast and orange juice, "Expensive trinkets are fine, but I still don't feel like my efforts have been adequately compensated."

"What would do it for you?" asked Tim, a little forlorn and quite embarrassed at the thought of facing the lobster again.

"How about a three month tour of the continent?" she answered in a snap. "All the great cities. And a chauffeured limosine to take us around, of course."

Tim stumbled a bit on his way back to the boat, but it was reticence this time, not clumsiness. He really didn't feel right about asking any more of the lobster. He was deeply ashamed at human greed.

Feeling more than a little uxorious, Tim roused the lobster by singing the lyrics to a few songs from Broadway musicals, ("Stranger in Paradise" did it, actually), and as usual when he asked for the latest wish, it was granted immediately and Tim was able to cruise home in his boat quite confidently, though he did a little minor damage to the hull when he hit the side of his berth when trying to moor. He had the boat repaired, over-hauled and painted while they were in Europe. They had a splendid time: it was like a second honeymoon. Romance between Tim and Joanne was rekindled for the first time in years.

"You know, honey," she said, naked under a sheet in a hotel in Calais, "I've enjoyed this trip, and I love my marquis-cut, and my sable, but I've had it all wrong about that lobster."

"I'm glad to hear you say that," said Tim, pouring himself a cognac and reaching into his robe pocket for his pipe.

"Yes. I thought material things would bring meaning to my existence, but now that I have them I see that there's something much more important missing from our lives."

Tim broke the wooden match he was attempting to strike, and he reached in the box for another. Out of the pipeless side of his mouth he said, "What's that, dear?"

"Children," she said blissfully, staring at the hand-carved cornices. "The minute we get home, I want you to go out and tell that lobster to do whatever he has to do to get you going: he has to conjure us up a family one way or the other."

"Perhaps you're a bit old to get pregnant."

67

"Well, tell him to send us one already born, then. I don't care how he does it."

Of course, it happened just as before. Tim invoked the lobster by reading Elizabethan sonnets out loud, and he wished for a family and the lobster told him to go home to it. There was a boy and a girl, both healthy, good-looking, and well-behaved. The four of them enjoyed many outings to the beach, to the mountains, to the city. It was idyllic for a while and Tim thought Joanne would at last be satisfied, but inevitably he underestimated the trenchant discontent that ruled her existence.

"It's not all it's cracked up to be," she told Tim one Sunday night after a weekend picnic and camp-out on the beach. "There's got to be more to life than this. All I do as a mother is give, give, give. It's like I have three of you instead of just one to nurture. I feel even more frustrated than before. A family doesn't fulfill my life, it empties it even more."

"Well, perhaps you should give it a little more time," suggested Tim, trying to put soothing cream on his sunburned face.

"No. I've been thinking it over all day. What would make me most happy is to have an identity of my own, a reason for being, a frame of reference for myself in the universe. If I were a corporate Chairman of the Board, or better yet, someone powerful in government. That's it! Go back to that lobster and have him make me a senator from Maine. Senior would be better, with a chairmanship of some powerful committee; let's make it Ways and Means."

"Ways and Means," repeated Tim.

The next morning he took off in his boat for the lobster beds with great sadness. He tried to invoke the magic lobster but it took quite a while: nothing worked this time until he started singing opera lyrics. His voice was very poor and colorless, but the poignance matched his feeling when he sang the sad lament of Madame Butterfly. It finally brought the lobster up.

"What is it now?" said the lobster.

"Well, I have another wish," said Tim, having to hold himself steady by hanging on to the boat rail. "But first, I wonder if I could ask you something?"

"Sure," said the lobster.

Tim grinned foolishly. "Well, I was just wondering how you decide which invocation to respond to. Is it something ordained by magic, too? I'm nearly out of things to try, and if there's a pattern to it, I'd like to know. Not that I think I'll need to bother you again, I know you've done more than enough. I hope I'm not wearing out your capacity to fulfill wishes. But it's just out of curiosity, more than anything else. Why does it take different rhymes or lyrics to rouse you every time?"

The lobster answered quickly, and impatiently, "It's the twentieth century, Bud. In the earlier times we only needed one particular chant, always the same and which always worked. But these days with our insatiable lust for novelty, I have to have something new every time."

"Oh," said Tim, thoughtfully. "It makes sense."

"You should have been able to figure it out for yourself."

Tim smiled. "But, anyway, I do have a wish this time. My wife wants to be the senior senator from Maine with the chairmanship of the Ways and Means Committee."

"About time she got around to being something," quipped the lobster.

"Or at least, becoming something," added Tim.

"Go on home," said the lobster.

"Thanks a lot," said Tim. "You know I really appreciate . . ."

"Go on home."

As usual, Tim returned home to find the wish fulfilled. Now Joanne was so busy she had no time for the family and no time either to think about her own meaninglessness, or of the future. Tim had to take care of the kids and the house. She was gone most of the time, and truth to tell, Tim sort of liked the boy and girl and didn't miss his wife much. He gave up lobstering as a profession, not as a sacrifice, but more with relief, since they could all live comfortably on her salary. They kept the boat, though, and used it now for pleasure.

But, after a few months, Joanne came home exhausted. "I need a rest," she moaned.

"Shall I go ask the lobster?" grinned Tim.

She wasn't even slightly amused. She glared at him. "You could have come to Washington with me to help. The kids could have been put in good schools. Now because of my fidelity and industriousness, I'm completely alone and tired and in need of good company. That's what we'll go discuss with your lobster."

Tim looked at the floor and saw that the carpet needed to be vacuumed.

They left the kids with a babysitter, and they both climbed into Tim's boat to go out to the lobster beds, as she demanded. This time the lobster appeared without invocation, ("Just to throw you off") and Joanne reached down to the water to pluck him up. Hoping that he would turn into a handsome prince, she kissed him, but nothing at all happened.

"Probably wore him out with all your wishes," remarked Tim, nearly slipping off the deck in a slight swell.

Joanne glared at Tim, then insisted on taking the lobster back with them. When they reached land she told Tim it was all over between them, and then she and the lobster ran away to Italy.

Tim was rather glad to be rid of her, and he did have his kids to keep him company. Being a practical and forgiving man, he went about his business as before and tried to overlook the shortcomings of humans.

RAPUNZEL

Real Theme: Fundamentalism

Rapunzel Matthews was born in Missouri and was named that because her mother was an avid salad eater, mainly as an effort to lose weight. Mrs. Matthews knew that for a name, Lettuce or Watercress just wouldn't do. At first she was going to call her daughter the minimally acceptable Romaine, but then she read a reference to the old tale which explained that Rapunzel was another name for Rampion, so there it was. Mrs. Matthews would do anything to sound or seem more European: a European name was far superior to an American one. Mr. Matthews was chauvinistically American, but as such was always thinking about money, so he had very little to say about naming the child.

Of course, in reality, Rapunzel's parents were good egalitarian Americans, even if their ancestors were Northern European immigrants, so the peccadillo of their daughter's name could be forgiven as ancestor worship. However, as good Americans, they naturally thought they were entitled to a

71

surfeit of everything available in consumer goods. "Those other countries didn't win World War II," her father would perpetually snarl, "American blood earned us the right to lead the Western World. As the leaders we deserve the best. American sweat made the bullets that killed the Krauts and Japs."

Never a stickler for accuracy, Rapunzel's father, whose first name was Marv, was employed by the state. He was one of those numerous obscure petty administrators with an ambiguous title like "Director of Project Analyses" or "Head of Status of Facilities Report Unit," and he typically could be found sitting at the dinner table complaining about high taxes, inflation, low pay, or the like. Rapunzel's mother, Amanda, was also quite typical; she was a stay-at-home mother who with a long-suffering sigh could express the essence of her being while ironing long-sleeved white shirts in front of a talk show or a Dialing-for-Dollars movie on TV.

Quite naturally Rapunzel was alienated from her parents' way of life the minute she realized how often children follow in their parents' footsteps. "Not for me," she decided, loathing her suburban life outside Kansas City. At seventeen she bought herself an acoustic guitar, and with her own natural ability to play music (she had played "America the Beautiful" by ear on her brother's trumpet when she was six and he was eight, something that caused him, being stuck on scales still, to give up the instrument in envy and despair) and to sing, she took off for downtown Kansas City to break the chains and routines of her tedious and stifling background and begin her own career.

This was 1970. With her long straight brown hair and her compelling high cheekbones, albeit a large nose, she was perfect as a folk singer. First she modeled herself on Joan Baez, and Buffy St. Marie; later she advanced to Judy Collins and Joni Mitchell. She got involved with a bassist named Ishmael who brought out her repressed sensuality and introduced her to the obligatory drugs for a musical career. Then he told her she needed to leave this area she had grown up in and set out into the real world if she ever expected to make it.

Without a thought she followed his advice. She went to Florida and sang on the streets to get money to buy food. She was running into a recurring problem though: she was just a little too late for the folk singing craze of the sixties, too late by about five years in each phase she entered. Art songs were big, and originality, too, but she didn't have an ounce of creative talent, only a nice voice and her somewhat pitiful sex appeal. It wasn't really enough for a serious career.

"Rapunzel, Rapunzel, let down your hair," all her lovers would say, since she piled it in a coil on top of her head most of the time because it got in her way when it was down. It was annoying. Often she would catch a few hairs in a chair back, or in the splinter of a wooden bench, which caused her much pain to pull it; or she would catch a tress in the string of a guitar if she wasn't careful. But she couldn't bring herself to cut it, as though something religious rebelled in her at the thought of wearing short hair.

In Florida she met Harlan Peevey, two years younger than she was, while he was stationed in the navy at Pensacola. He was at this time regularly taking heavy doses of hallucinogens in order to get a medical discharge from the service. Eventually it worked: he was judged unfit for military service; he was too crazy to go to Vietnam and fight. He agreed in principle that if Vietnam was sane, he was the opposite. After a few nights in the rooms of friends he'd met, he signed on with a few other young men who were driving a van to Washington State, where he had some other friends. She had heard it was beautiful there, so she just tagged along. Harlan was nice to her; that was enough. Rapunzel only had a knapsack of clothes and her guitar in its case. She made herself useful to the others because they could stop on city streets or in parks along the way, and she could sing with the case open and make a few dollars for gas or groceries.

They reached Tacoma on a beautiful June day, and they moved into a house with the other members of the van party and Harlan's friends, a couple from Wisconsin. Everyone quickly applied for food stamps, and among them all they made the low rent and utilities with a minimum of working time, which was nice since they all hated to work. Often drug deals helped with the finances.

Rapunzel's life slowly began to change in this time. It was no witch who locked her up in a tower, but a woman several years older than she who converted Rapunzel to fundamentalism. Rapunzel met Teresa while they were both working as temporary office help. The relationship continued and was indeed a fertile one. From anti-war counterculture and pseudo-atheism, they evolved through chanting cults, pseudo-scientific parapsychological nonsense, and any other titillating psychic fad that tantalized their so-called minds. Not surprisingly, and along with a multitude of other ex-hippies, they ended up with the kind of Christianity that takes the Bible absolutely literally, written by divinely inspired men as though by God's own hand, and interpreted correctly today only by His chosen charismatics. With each step in her spiritual odyssey, Rapunzel would somehow find herself in the position to let down her hair, and the more she did, it seemed, the more she learned. When she reached the ultimate truth, she learned that there was no error in the Bible, no inconsistency in fact or actual occurrence. It was all absolutely true, the *manna* from heaven was literally that, the miracles just as described: the works. If one couldn't understand it, there was something wrong with one's understanding.

Naturally everyone with an IQ in three figures could see Rapunzel and Teresa had the glaring fault of stupidity, but the existential era of mankind couldn't even boast of better educational techniques or less ignorance. The girls had to read their Absolute Authority in a watered down version worded in such basic terms that all the poetry and inspiration were gone. All the nuances of the human spiritual dilemmas were lost on them, all the depth incomprehensible. They had no ability to debate the issues though they argued about it all the time with anyone available. Rapunzel once scored a verbal victory in the old argument over inconsistency in names in the genealogies of Luke and Matthew. When challenged about the two different names given to Joseph's father, she suggested, "Maybe he *had* two names." This very psychedelic way of handling religion should have been expected of one whose brain cells had been so abused. But Rapunzel was sincere: she attended several different churches and ended up with one where the main dogma became political, where abortion, women's rights, school busing, and book censorship were the issues closest to God, therefore the most important to her.

The disco craze was in full swing now, and Rapunzel had her hair done in little braids. But she leaned more to country-western, then to hymns: someone had put all the psalms to music, complete with guitar chords.

Soon, like most mindless obsessives or obsessive compulsives, Rapunzel convinced herself that the end was near. She disdained the temptation and hard work of building an ark, or at least a fallout shelter. She was brought to believe that her salvation consisted in some mystical notion that Jesus Christ was going to swoop down from heaven, presumably on wings, and gather in his literal arms all his faithful while the rest of humanity deservedly perished in hellfires of damnation, that is, thermonuclear war. No other historical period posed this threat: Rapunzel's historical comprehension was sadly insufficient. Before the present era all was bucolic and Edenic: now was the day of judgment. To her "ancient history" meant last year.

She lost herself in campaigns to take *Ms.* magazine off high school shelves because articles in it mentioned the word orgasm, which when she thought about it, was an inferior word to the clean and puritanical "climax." She argued for the right to carry hand guns, for the sale of public lands, for prayer in school, in short, anything the church advocated. This made her feel blissful, blessed, and protected, with her salvation assured.

At the same time this spiritual metamorphosis was going on in Rapunzel, all the roommates were slowly moving out on their own, and in 1975 Harlan was forced to get a regular job. Rapunzel was pregnant to boot. She tried to pick up her guitar, but more and more "The Circle Game" and "Both Sides Now" seemed passé, even blasphemous. All she could get out of herself was a reedy and pathetic "Amazing Grace." She and Harlan decided to get married, just for the sake of the baby. Locked up in the dungeon of a house in a bad neighborhood of a dingy town, she became very depressed. Even "Gone the Rainbow" was unequal to her gloom.

Teresa, the witch, as some people actually did call her because she was always referring to occult subjects and practices and was making absurd coincidences into a proof of ESP while discussing nothing but auras, fortune-telling, etc., had by now become the major influence in Rapunzel's life. Soon it was 1978 and Rapunzel had two little girls to think about. Her parents visited her, and when they saw the dumpy house, they immediately arranged to give Harlan and Rapunzel money for a down payment on a house of their own, but only on one condition: they had to move back to Kansas City. The young couple did, of course, Harlan being abysmally lazy and glad to take a job his father-in-law could get him with the state. At the same time Teresa mysteriously moved back to her original home town, Ottumwa, Iowa.

Rapunzel was terribly disillusioned with life as a wife and mother. She and Harlan had argued violently at first, but now they just agreed they were only staying together for the sake of the children. Rapunzel was often seen at sleazy bars on the outskirts of town, and she began to wear heavy makeup, trying to be attractive, even though her nose and her chin were gradually reaching towards each other year by year. She trusted in God to forgive her for her sexual indiscretions, which she was earnestly trying to quit. But any time someone repeated the magic words, "Rapunzel, Rapunzel, let down your hair," she was a pushover. Harlan tortured her about this, at first because he was jealous but then just out of disgust, calling her "slut."

To add to her woes, her first boyfriend and lover was still around, and she couldn't help dreaming about what her life would have been like had she not left at all. He was the only one she ever had simultaneous orgasms with. She thought, "No wonder I'm not satisfied."

Harlan, as fate will have it, was an avowed atheist, and he cruelly exposed her hypocrisy, teased her about her lame-brained Christianity, openly told people how she would say and do whatever fitted her yen for the moment, and that she really didn't care about anyone, which was true. He stayed with her to keep her from abusing the children, since the way she screamed at them was supernaturally severe. He was afraid she would go insane, or he would: perhaps the navy had been right in their assessment that he was mentally unfit. Anyone who could get himself in this situation was questionable.

So, the Hell they had created for themselves just continued on with no resolution. Rapunzel visited Teresa in Iowa as much as possible, and they kept in close touch by writing letters. Often Teresa would send her chain letters and unsigned enigmatic greeting cards. They could always "Sense" each other's presence and they planned to move in together when the kids were grown. This disgusted Harlan, but whenever he forbade Rapunzel to go to bars or to see Teresa, even using the Bible's commandment that the wife obey the husband, Rapunzel just laughed at him and said, "We weren't married in the Church, so it really doesn't count."

As time went on and times got more and more materialistic and superficial, she drifted into consumer indulgence. Harlan was doing all right in his job, so she bought a microwave oven, and they soon put up an aboveground swimming pool. She relied more and more on objects and platitudes to get her by, and the last anyone ever heard of her, she had gotten rid of her guitar and bought a ghetto blaster.

HENNEY PENNEY

Real Theme: Nuclear Dread

Henrietta was one of those unfortunate children of vulgar parents who name their offspring as a joke. Her father was related at some distance to the J.C. Penney who founded the department store chain, but the connection was worth no more than an executive position with the chain. Henney was laughed at from the minute she was introduced to anyone and could never get anyone to take her seriously, though she had always been a concerned and serious person. She could have changed her name, but she decided to wait until she got married; that would take care of it, and in the meantime it wasn't right to be overly concerned with trivialities. She had, in fact, transcended the stigma by the time she got to college and turned into a Late-Sixties Idealist, (they were known in the early days of the movement as Flower Children). Unfortunately the year was 1974.

U.C. Berkeley still had political rallies and speeches in Sproul Plaza, with tables set up filled with pamphlets and lists of activities, but the generations had changed in a decade and Mid-Seventies Conformism had supplanted the radicals. Henney was an anachronism, at least five years too late in an intellectual fashion-world that depends on split-seconds in timing for effectiveness and influence. So when Henney wanted to start an anti-nuclear weapons group on campus, she was discouraged from it, not with arguments and rational debate, but with Me-Decade apathy.

Henney had a form of existential dread that is common enough (and on the increase), but it is so near pathological that no one likes to admit it and be taken for an obsessive neurotic, or worse, a neurotic obsessive. Nuclear Dread is identified by the excessive terror created by the sound of a jet plane up in the sky. Henney felt the passing of a jet as an all-encompassing rumble in the skies, as if there were no other event going on at the moment. She'd look up in the sky when the horrible thunder of a jet plane filled the air, and she'd watch it go overhead with the uncontrollable sensation: "This is it."

She told a friend about the Dread. She figured she was crazy, or half-crazy, and asked him if he thought she was ready for the couch yet. He said she wasn't the only one who had the symptoms of ND. Lots of people had nightmares about the aftermath of a nuclear war, or of an air raid that gave the world ten minutes left to exist. He said it was just something in the collective unconscious, and he recommended she take some positive action: join a group, write a pamphlet, or picket an Air Force base.

With all she saw around her, Henney felt those forms of activism were a bit too mundane and probably wouldn't attract much attention. She needed something more esoteric: quotidian things were not her style. She advertised in the *Daily Cal* for participants in a summer "Ride to Washington D.C." to protest nuclear weapons. She took several months to line up the members of the ride, who had to bring their own ten-speeds and donate a share towards the rental of a van to transport equipment, tents, sleeping bags, and anyone who got tired. Henney mapped out the course herself, after sending to a cycling club for brochures and then reading all the back issues of magazines for tips and information.

She chose the group carefully, taking into account health, maturity, and dedication to the cause, as well as ability to contribute money, which some of them admittedly had in their favor to a high degree. One of the first to be chosen was the heir to the Lucky's Supermarket fortune. Ducky Lucky was a Piedmont product who could have single-handedly bought the anti-nuclear lobby from his own wallet. He was a surprisingly quiet being, and when Henney asked him his personal feelings about the issue—like did he want his children to be mutants—he avoided giving concrete answers or getting too worked up about it, leading Henney to suspect he was afflicted with Dread and couldn't even confront the issue directly. He said he wanted to go because he didn't want to have to play tennis again all summer.

Turkey Lurkey was a more dedicated member of the group. He was from Hayward and was not particularly a social asset, since he looked like he belonged in a cartoon strip: dark shaggy hair, large thick glasses with dark plastic rims, large nose, ludicrous smile that was close-lipped to hide the irregularly planted teeth. He was thin and short and just looked funny. But he worked hard distributing leaflets to publicize the ride, and he was persuasive in speaking against the nuclear fallout possibilities and the dangers of radioactivity.

To balance the group, Henney chose the popular athlete, Cocky Locky, whose fan club would make up the crowds at the point of embarkation and along the route. Cocky was on an athletic scholarship and was a celebrity in the West already. He had to be back early, he told Henney, to start training for football season: this was the year he thought he was going to get the Heismann. He was a charming person, if a bit predictable, but a good media draw, and it's to be suspected that Henney herself had a bit of a crush on him.

Goosey Poosey, the renowned East Oakland streetwalker, who could be found any afternoon at the corner of MacArthur and East 14th in those days, had requested admittance to the group, and though some authors have included her in their versions of the tale, the true facts are that Henney would never have associated with such trash, though she would also never have said it that way; she made an appropriate excuse to Goosey: the van was full already, or they were limited to four.

Anyway, they started out from Sather Gate on June 15, intending to ride an average of seventy to a hundred miles a day. There were only a few people, and all of them friends or admirers of Cocky, who crowded around them as they took off in a Southeast direction, intending to brave the heat of the desert rather than try to surmount the heights of mountains. They rode hard and pulled into the first stopover a little east of Fresno, where they set up camp and built a fire to barbeque hamburgers. Then they all took showers in the campground facilities and set up their own tents and sleeping bags. Cocky and Turkey both slept out in the open, but the rest had their own personal little tents.

Henney felt very pleased and content with the first day's progress. They had made it as far as she had planned without a flat tire or any other mishap. She tried to think out the next leg of the journey in her mind, but she was exhausted from all the exercise and fell asleep the minute she hit the sleeping bag.

Foxy Loxy lived in Fresno and he had heard on the radio about the protest ride. As a publicized event, it was drawing a few waves from people, but there wasn't the local coverage Henney had hoped for when she sent letters and notices to newspapers and radio stations along the way: there were token announcements, but the only reporter they had seen had just wanted to interview Cocky about his plans for playing in the NFL.

Foxy Loxy was a dropout from a local community college, and when he heard about the group on the ride he became inspired with a plan. He followed them on his Honda Trail 90 at a distance so they wouldn't see him, and when they bedded down for the night he found a hiding place in some nearby caves, and he parked his motorcycle there.

It is to be debated what Foxy's motives were in this tragedy. Was he the incarnation of evil? Was he the cosmic balance? The universal wrench in the works? Was he an isolated individual moved by a private problem or part of a conspiracy by plutonium importers, the AEC, or Conservatives, any of which could have hired him?

Psychiatrists, theorizing after the crime, disagreed on whether Foxy was a vicious pathological killer or just another misguided victim of nuclear neurosis, which had temporarily lapsed into psychosis that fateful night. This is what happened:

Foxy put a knife to Turkey's throat and stuffed a rag into his mouth, simultaneously waking him up and warning him to be silent. Then he tied Turkey's arms and led him up to the caves above the camp. There he slowly and sadistically murdered the poor Turkey, dismembering him cruelly and piling the parts in different corners of the cave. Next, Foxy sneaked up on the snoring Ducky and again without waking the others, managed to get him up to the cave, where he again cut his victim up into parts piled into particular corners. Cocky Locky was the hardest to subdue, because he was stronger and could easily have overpowered Foxy at any time. The autopsy revealed that Cocky's skull had been crushed by some large object, probably a rock. His body was then dragged to the cave, and separated into pieces like the others.

Fortunately the night's work had taken up almost all the hours of darkness, and the sun was beginning to lighten up the eastern border of the sky. Cocky had made a sound just before having his head bashed in, and Henney had peeked out of the tent just in time to witness Foxy dragging the muscular body away. When they were out of sight, she jumped on her ten-speed and made it to the ranger's station in a few moments. One of the rangers was just getting up and he saw the frenzied Henney jump off her bike, letting it fall to the ground, and run up to him frantically. She could hardly talk, she was in such a state, but the ranger managed to realize she was talking about a killer, and he quickly called the police.

The Fresno city police, the county sheriff, and the California Highway Patrol had arrived by the time the whole story was being understood. The authorities surrounded Foxy Loxy while he was still in his caves, and through a loudspeaker they commanded him to surrender himself at once. He didn't respond, so they threatened to use tear gas to get him out. The campground was being evacuated, and when it was empty, the gas masks were distributed to the police and the caves were bombed with gas. Then, with rifles up, and gas masks on, they moved in on Foxy, advancing to the cave where they expected to find him. Then they had to wait until the wind cleared away the tear gas so they could locate the cave and rush him.

They, of course, hadn't needed to use such extreme tactics. Foxy Loxy had stabbed himself in the stomach and fallen over Ducky Lucky's disembodied legs. When the police found the cave, they were shocked and disgusted. An ambulance was called and Foxy was kept alive by transfusions and twelve hours of surgery at the city hospital. He stayed in a coma for three months and when he was conscious enough to stand trial, he was examined for the court by a team of psychiatrists, whose diagnoses ranged from "nothing wrong" to acute mania and paranoid psychosis. The jury found him guilty of three counts of first degree murder and he was sentenced to life imprisonment, but he died the next week of pneumonia that had set in after he had been moved out of the hospital and into the drafty courtroom. The doctors said there was nothing they could do to save him because he was so weakened by this time.

Foxy's defense attorney had tried to show that Foxy was mentally deficient, but the Fresno jury didn't believe it. Foxy might have gotten off if the trial had been moved to another city, the lawyer told the newspapers. The technicalities of the arrest could have been made a case of, since in the confusion over who had jurisdiction—city, county, or state—no one had read Foxy his rights as they waited for the ambulance. True, he was passed out in a puddle of his own blood, but an adequate defense could have preserved Foxy's civil rights.

Henney, naturally, was never the same afterwards. She tried to resume her studies, but somehow her zest and ambition were gone. For a while she tried to organize against Nuclear Power Plants, saying that it had been a poor management decision in the Fifties and sooner or later we would just have to cut our losses and dismantle what we already had and go with alternative energy sources, but her heart wasn't in it. She did lose her Nuclear Dread, but began to be afraid of going into public, especially alone. The state provided her with some psychiatric help to aid her in coping with the trauma, but she found it impossible to vote, to use the public services, and to depend on the police or courts for protection against other maniacal people.

In the end she became addicted to prescription drugs and got involved with some unsavory characters from the lower side of Telegraph Avenue. The last anyone heard of her, she was travelling around in a bus with the drummer of a small-time jazz band.

85

THE COUNTRY MOUSE
AND THE CITY MOUSE

Real Theme: Dietary Purity

The main thing to clear up about this fairy tale is that the two principals were not mice, but rats. Walter lived in the Santa Cruz mountains, in a small cabin provided to him by a grandparent, who had not died but who was too old to hike the three miles of slopes to get to the place, and who wanted to hang onto the property for a couple more years before selling it, since the property value was appreciating rapidly enough to keep pace with inflation. Walter lived there, apart from civilization and eschewing its crowds, but indulging himself in whatever habits came easily. He bathed irregularly, kept the cabin dirty and messy, and ate whatever was easiest to reach. There was no electricity to the cabin, so he couldn't use appliances, and he was too lazy to carry propane for a refrigerator, so he couldn't store any perishables. He did cook on the wood burning stove until the pot became disabled for further use because he couldn't force himself to clean his dishes. He ended up walking the six miles to and from the little town on the highway to buy prepared food more often than he liked, but since he only planned day to day he didn't really notice it. At first he had eaten in the town's two restaurants, but he was living off savings from his last job as a parcel delivery man and he didn't want to spend his money too fast. Before this time he had always had a poor diet, eating in fast food restaurants, and besides that he habitually smoked Pall Mall cigarettes.

His cousin, Harold, lived in San Francisco and worked in a natural foods store. Most of the employees worked there to be in an alternative lifestyle because they were alienated from the cheapness and artificiality of modern life manifested in its foods. Harold knew the owner of the store, so he managed to land a full-time job that gave him enough money to live on, as well as the free vegetables, fruits, whole-grain flour, raw milk and cheese, honey, nuts, seeds, and all the rest of the healthy, unprocessed, organic, nutritious products the contemporary responsible eaters desired. Harold lived in a homemade camper on the back of a Studebaker pick-up that he parked in various driveways and parking lots in order to avoid paying rent in any permanent place, since who were rats to claim ownership to any part of the earth?

Harold was dark and thin, though he ate prodigiously. He wore contact lenses, and he always looked bulgy-eyed, as though something surprising were happening; perhaps the lenses irritated his eyes or made them appear larger or deeper than they were. His cheekbones were high and his nose was sharp, not rounded quite enough to prevent his face from having a severe expression, as though he were sitting in judgment on vital cases. He had worked at the natural foods store for three years, and as his clothes wore out, one of the employees, a young female named Abigail, also thin and gaunt, sewed him shirts and pants so that his clothing became as personal and organic as his diet. He believed in eating meat and she was a vegetarian, so the affair was doomed.

87

Walter was burly and blond with kinky tight curls that looked so bad when they got long that he always kept scissors around so he could cut his hair himself, because a barber was so expensive, with the result that the cut was always uneven and lop-sided and he perpetually looked shaggy and unkempt. He had always had a slight weight problem, but walking to the town from his cabin, and back again, with a bag full of donuts, cupcakes, potato chips, and whatever else he could find that wouldn't spoil for a few days had counteracted the caloric effects of those foods, and he had only a small paunch for a stomach to belie his sloth and gluttony. He wore hightop Converse tennis shoes, no socks, and his other clothing came from the Goodwill or Salvation Army stores.

With so much free time it's no surprise that both of them were great readers in contemporary literature. Both had been into Eastern mysticism and philosophy at the same time, and both had decided the world was, after all, existential, and they had no course in it but to be there in the world until it ended, which seemed inevitable some time or other in the future if not globally, at least for their own personal selves or until, in Walter's case, he had to get a job and go to work again.

Harold's "weekends" were on Wednesday and Thursday, so he often drove down to visit Walter; they went to the Santa Cruz Boardwalk to watch the people and compare the rides in the amusement park to different metaphysical phenomena: the roller coaster as a symbol of modern political commitment, the ferris wheel as the cycle of birth and death and rebirth. Walter, at these times, ate ice cream bars he bought at concession stands, and Harold ate oranges and nectarines he brought from the store. They usually watched for a while, mainly in silence, and then walked along the ocean, letting the waves wet their feet, without trying to influence the course of existence by getting out of the way. Then they would talk about life and existence, analyzing the follies of modern rats and berating the value of quotidian monotony.

One day Harold peeled an orange and tried to force it on Walter.

"I don't like fruit," said Walter. "It gives me the runs."

"That's only because your body is so speeded up on all that processed sugar," said Harold patiently. "It has to work so hard to digest all those carbohydrates and saturated fats that when it gets to a little natural sugar, it goes into shock. But once you got used to it, you'd normalize."

Walter glared at him. "I have no intention whatever of getting used to it."

The waves almost reached their feet.

"Do you know how bad your veins and arteries will be after all that junk food?" said Harold, somewhat dispassionately. "If you don't die of a heart attack or cancer from the chemicals and preservatives, you'll die a slow suffocating death from arteriosclerosis. And your lungs! Now you're young enough that it doesn't matter, but think of when you're forty or fifty. Then is when it catches up with you." Even as Harold made his case, it was obvious he felt guilty for being so bombastic and interfering with someone else's life.

"I'm not going to live every minute of my life in anxiety," said Walter, simply and with dignity. "The doctors don't know everything. Science is fallible: that's been proven often enough."

Harold was obsessive about it, though. "Proper nutrition could be the answer to all our medical needs: diabetes, blood pressure, bad teeth, insomnia, anything." They had begun walking again. "A poor diet may be responsible for depression. Life may not be that bad, after all."

They reached the pier and turned around to walk back to where the truck was parked. Walter stretched the limits of his patience and said, "You don't think it's all that great, either. And you have a fibrous diet."

"Well, that's different," said Harold. "My depression is ideological."

"Maybe you ought to take up a bad habit." Walter saw that he had hurt his cousin's feelings, so he tried to soothe him by eating a few pieces of celery with dehydrogenated peanut butter.

They returned to the truck and drove back into the hills. When they came to the store nearest the cabin, Walter told Harold to stop and park across the street in back of the restaurant. Harold had not brought enough food to last both days, so he went into the store, too. When Walter bought a bag full of canned beans, tamales, soups, and spaghetti, Harold refused to help him carry it back up to the cabin. Harold bought a bag of unsalted peanuts and a quart of non-fat milk. They hiked the three miles to the cabin in an hour and a half. It was quiet, and a few harmless squirrels crossed the path in front of them. They got to the cabin and sat outside under a tall pine tree to watch the sun go down.

Then it was time for dinner. Walter opened a can of hot chili beans, extra spicy, and ate it cold from the can. This took away any trace of hunger which Harold had been feeling, but he drank his lukewarm milk and cracked a few nuts, being sure to put the shells in a bag so as not to leave any more garbage on the earth. Walter also didn't leave his garbage strewn through the wilderness; he threw it in a heap under a few bushes not far from his front door, and every time he went down to the store he tried to carry a bag of trash out with him to empty it there.

They turned on the battery-operated light in the cabin and took out their books. Walter was reading *Being and Nothingness* in translation and Harold was reading *Being and Time* in the original. Harold had considered doing a translation to bring his favorite author to greater availability, but they didn't pay well enough for him to make that kind of effort.

At one point in the evening Walter looked up, caught Harold's eye, and said, "It's a wonder we still bother to read." Then he opened a package of powdered-sugar donuts. He didn't offer one to Harold but chewed several, half a circle at a time, leaving white dust down the front of his shirt.

Harold watched but didn't answer, not because he disagreed, but because he didn't feel the issue was significant enough to debate. He kept on reading, reclined on his sleeping bag with his back to the lamp, letting the light over his shoulder onto the book and wondering whether the batteries were running down or if it was just his imagination that made it seem like the light was getting dimmer and dimmer.

Sometime later in the evening, when Walter lit a Pall Mall, Harold looked up angrily. "I wish you wouldn't smoke in a closed room with me. It's very inconsiderate. It forces me to breathe in the smoke and that's as bad as smoking, according to the latest tests."

Walter put the cigarette out with excessive ceremony. He was lounging on his bed, a mattress on a box spring, set on some boards so it was off the floor, but with no space under it for a mop or a broom.

Harold was intent on his book, but Walter soon grew restless. "What do you think are the odds of getting this place willed to us when the old man dies?"

Harold kept his place with his thumb and shrugged. "We're the only grandchildren. I think there are a couple of grandnieces or nephews on the other side of the family. He'll probably outlive both of us though, so why worry about it?"

"What do you mean?"

"He wasn't brought up on television, Sugar Pops, and Tang."

"Of course." Walter sighed. "I suppose I'll have to get a job one of these days. Then probably a girlfriend. Maybe a car, or worse—a house with a mortgage, a family, charge accounts."

Harold sat quietly. Actually, why should those things be any different with Walter's present life if he didn't make them that way? Then there was nothing on his mind so he sat silently and waited.

Neither was there anything on Walter's mind. In part he wanted to appear compelling and significant to Harold, so Harold would admire him and consider him either heroic or anti-heroic. But in part he only wanted another donut and a cigarette.

Harold soon fell asleep over his book. Walter opened two windows to get a crosscurrent and sat up smoking pensively and staring at the stars over the tops of the pines. He was considering something abstract that Sartre had said about morals, but the meaning was fading as he meditated on it, and he wasn't sure there was any point in formulating a counter-expository discussion in his own mind. Finally he too went to sleep.

A scraggly wild black cat with yellow eyes went through Walter's garbage just as the sun was coming up, but nobody saw him or heard him. Harold woke up early, before Walter, and hiked back to the highway in a hurry to get home for some herb tea.

THE THREE LITTLE PIGS

Real Theme: Political Idealism

There were actually children in the world when this story first came to prominence, but of course in this generation those born without mature minds are doomed to oblivion: some two and three year olds teach themselves how to read, others commit suicide once they realize the competition. They have no use these days for the lies the average child needed to be told in the past. So the stories surrounding the lives of the three little pigs certainly need a retelling suitable for modern times, with truth being the purpose of the telling and not the propagation of hope-filled illusions such as integrating the personality or overcoming destructive forces.

The three little pigs in "The Three Little Pigs" were three brothers who were born each a year apart in a suburb of Birmingham, Alabama. When the oldest brother, Edmund, was twenty-five, a magic spirit came to him out of nowhere and told him he could have any wish he wanted.

Edmund thought about it a bit, then said, "Why me?"

The spirit replied, "No reason; it was an utterly arbitrary decision. Most supernatural decisions are, you know."

Edmund said, "No, I didn't."

The spirit returned, "Well, next year I'll do the same for your brother Eugene, and the year after that for your brother Homer."

Edmund then asked, "How can I believe you?"

The spirit didn't answer but only hovered about enigmatically. Edmund thought it over for a little while. The only thing he had truly been desiring was for his life to have some purpose, some project that would make getting out of bed in the morning a little easier. He'd had a few jobs and thought about having a family or going into the Army, but the effort appeared to be disproportionate to the rewards. He'd considered college, but there was no money in it. He'd had an altruistic period where he'd hung out in front of the Goodwill store, considering volunteering for a job, but that fell through, too.

What he really wanted to do with his life was to sit in an office high up in some building, perhaps in downtown Birmingham, and make fifty thousand a year for doing nothing. As the oldest brother he was good at telling people what to do, so he thought he'd make a perfect business executive. He told this to the magic spirit and it said to him, "No problem, Ed; that's an easy wish, but I must warn you that gains easily gotten are easily lost." The spirit arched its eyebrows in a suggestive way.

"If it's the only way I'll get that kind of life, I'll take it," said the little pig. Actually he was 5'5", which wasn't all that little, *he* thought.

So Edmund inexplicably found himself on the twenty-eighth story of an insurance building, not in Birmingham, but in Atlanta, which was the only major city the firm had an opening in. In his office there was new modern furniture, and straw collages on the wall along with a few black and white photographs of city views. Out his window he could watch the goings-on at the Center for Disease Control, and he relished those possibilities, momentarily regretting that he hadn't thought to place his wish for a job there.

He walked over to his desk and saw the folders and papers on it, but no sooner had he sat down and begun shuffling through them than a courier arrived to take them and leave some others. Edmund enjoyed himself here for the rest of the afternoon and knew he would fit into the routine of corporate life quite well. The week passed quickly, and he amused himself by looking out the window and meditating on the cloud changes in the sky if nothing else was happening, and waiting for the courier to take a batch of papers and folders and leave a new batch. Sometimes Edmund even read through these pages and folders, but he couldn't make anything of the contents.

The wolf, Ralph, no relation to the wolf in "Little Red Riding Hood," happend by Edmund's office after the first week. The reason for this might have been Ralph's infallible instinct for the vunerable, it might have been intervention by the same divine source that sent the spirit, wanting to further complicate the matter, or it could have been a legitimate coincidence.

The door was open because by now Edmund was getting a little restless, wondering what he had to do to get a promotion. He was tired of looking out his window and wanted to watch anything that might be happening in the hall. Ralph just walked right in.

"Who are you and what do you want" oinked Edmund.

Being in appetite, Ralph quickly responded, "I'm the owner of the building, and I want to know what you're doing in this office. I have no record of it's being rented out."

"Well, if I told you how I got here you wouldn't believe it," Edmund said. "Anyway, the company would have done the renting. You should check with them."

"What I believe is that you are sitting here generating no work, producing nothing and taking money that someone else had to sweat for."

"You don't have to put it so crassly," said the somewhat shocked Edmund, but to no avail: the wolf walked over and ate him right up without the slightest twinge of conscience.

Eugene only read about the story, since the papers covered the grisly incident in customary vivid detail, including a long interview with the courier, who arrived just in time to witness the murder. Ralph, of course, escaped, and the police were still searching for him when the magic spirit visited the next brother, just as it said it would.

Eugene thought quickly when the spirit offered him any wish in his heart. Like Edmund, Eugene lacked focus in his life and had spent most of his twenty-four years in a quandary as to what to do for the rest of it. None of the possibilities seemed interesting enough. He, too, wanted to escape the dull similarities and cheapness of the suburban life, but he considered the mistake of his brother.

"All right," he finally said to the spirit. "I want to go to Atlanta, too, but I want to work on a commune where everything is shared and where I'll have to work to earn my way. I want to live in a naturalistic house that harmonizes my inner being with my environment, and I only want things that fill my needs and aren't excessive. I want to help others and give of myself."

Poof; there he was, the second little pig, who was honestly little at 5'2''; he found himself on a ladder in an organically grown peach orchard, harvesting the latest crop. He slaved there for ten days in a row, then continued working in the communal house, mopping the floors, washing the windows, and washing laundry by hand in a sink. The money generated by the sale of peaches and of handmade crafts was divided up between the members of the commune, but Eugene gave his share to charity.

He was soon exhausted from the hard work, and he began to lose weight from his sparse diet, mainly the leftovers of the others. Still, he thought, I'm an asset to humanity, doing good; I'm doing the right thing. That knowledge alone should be enough to keep me going.

Meanwhile his co-workers began to ignore him because he lectured them so self-righteously whenever he caught them goofing off on the job or filching money from the general fund. When one of them bought a large automobile and a color TV from inherited money, Eugene harassed him mercilessly, with lectures about selfishness and indulgence. Then, surreptitiously, without letting anyone even suspect and not fully admitting it to himself, Eugene began keeping more and more of his allotted pay. He began buying himself lobsters and champagne for dinner, and he bought himself a computerized chess game so he could play at night while he was alone.

Ralph was leaning on a lamp post when he noticed Eugene going into the boardinghouse. The wolf saw that Eugene was a loner, which would lessen the danger of getting caught. After the escapade in the skyscraper earlier in the year, Ralph had been on the lam, and his diet had been reduced to munching derelicts and bums down by the bus station. So he was ravenously hungry and, besides that, some strange mysterious force drove him to decide to make a meal out of Eugene. Even though the young pig was a bit thin, he looked as though he was gaining weight.

Ralph followed him one evening. Eugene stopped at the butcher for some T-bone steak and then at the shoestore, where he bought some armadillo skin cowboy boots. The wolf cornered him behind a tree as Eugene cut through the park on the way home.

"What are you after?" said Eugene.

"It ain't money," grunted Ralph. "Like you."

"You've got me all wrong. I'm not after material gain. I just think we should perform however we're able to and get rewarded with what we need."

"Who cares what you think." Ralph then sneered and opened his jaws. Eugene was a pile of porkchop bones in a matter of minutes. The wolf left Eugene's boots and clothes with the remains, but he also ate the T-bone steaks.

When the spirit visited Homer, the last remaining brother was quite suspicious, and justifiably. He said, "My brothers leave home, end up in Atlanta for some unknown reason, and shortly thereafter are savagely eaten by a mad wolf the police are unable to apprehend."

"That has nothing to do with me," said the spirit. "I'm only here to grant you whatever you wish."

This challenge intrigued Homer. "What did they do wrong?" he mused to himself. "There must be a way to beat this thing. If I wish something, it's got to be powerful enough to keep the wolf away from me. A strong, infallible scheme. Hmmmm."

"Hey, I don't have forever," said the spirit. "This is my last wish fulfillment for the century and I'm going to leave for the upper regions as soon as I'm done. So could you step it up a little?"

"Upper regions? Like heaven? Paradise?"

"Sure. Where else would I go?"

Homer snapped his fingers. "That's it!" The spirit didn't have its guard up and almost disappeared at the finger snap but managed to stay materialized by a rapid counter spell. Homer continued, "If all the religion business is true, all I need is for God to be on my side. He'll protect me from the wolf. O.K. Here's my wish. I wish to overthrow the government and take it over in the name of God. I won't become president, but I'll be in charge of everything that comes under the title: Next Thing To God, Homer. Of course, my position passes to my first born son when I die."

The spirit said, "One Divine Monarchy, coming right up. But let me warn you, they've been known to fail."

"Also to succeed," said Homer. "Anyway, let's just call it a Theocracy."

The next thing he knew, he was standing on a balcony with tens of thousands of cheering people below. He waved to them benevolently and then retired to his chambers.

"Now I'm safe," he thought. "This concrete building is guarded day and night by my followers. The wolf couldn't possibly get in."

It was true; Ralph couldn't get in, but when he heard that the brother of those two succulent meals he had lately devoured was also in Atlanta, it was an irresistible temptation to round out the threesome. He resorted to his tireless guile. The wolf sent Homer an invitation to debate religion in the lobby of City Hall, just to prove that the Theocracy wasn't totally against democracy. Ralph realized he'd probably be caught and tortured, but he couldn't help himself.

Homer read the invitation and chuckled. He did go to City Hall, but it was several hours earlier than the wolf had suggested. After a speech about the superiority of life devoted to God, well attended by supporters and people rounded up off the street by supporters, Homer returned to his quarters.

Ralph, who had been all this time in makeup, arrived at City Hall just in time to watch the crowds disperse. He cursed the bad luck, since eating Homer in view of several thousand people would have been a unique delight. But his mind worked on another way to fulfill his desire. He considered an attack on the concrete building that housed the third pig, but obviously it was impossible. He had to lure him out of it again.

"You are invited to deliver a benediction at the graduating ceremonies of the International Boy Scouts," read the next invitation. Homer again felt the wolf's paw behind this, but he couldn't resist making a fool of his enemy.

When Ralph arrived at the gymnasium where the invitation told Homer to go, he soon found out that Homer had been there, had given a speech about the importance of youth, again well-attended even though spontaneous this time, and then had had his robes kissed and his name shouted out in unison with cheers. It was too much. Ralph's indignation inspired him to come up with an even more deceitful plot. He wrote to Homer, telling him that a miraculous conversion had taken place.

This letter said that the wolf had seen the error of his ways and was now ready to be accepted into the faith. Would Homer himself deign to perform the rites, to prove that the breech between them was no more?

Homer considered the possibility that the wolf was lying, but the power of his position had distorted his judgment. He assumed that God had come to the wolf and made him repent. The weight of the responsibility of office had gone to Homer's head and made it soft. He set out to meet the wolf, to make peace with him and to unite all the world under the one true way that leads to perfection in all things.

The wolf had been living in an orchard outside the city limits. Homer arrived there with his entourage and called in a loud voice for the wolf to come and receive God's blessing. The wolf hung his head and approached Homer penitently and humbly.

With all the guards around, the wolf would have to make his move at precisely the right time. He had a switchblade hidden in his mouth disguised as a tooth, and when the holy pig reached out to touch the wolf's head, the wolf pretended to cover his mouth to clear his throat as if he were about to speak. In one motion, he grabbed Homer, produced the switchblade, and backed away from the guards, saying, "If you don't leave right now, he dies."

They backed off, knowing they couldn't survive without their leader. The wolf tied Homer into the cockpit of a waiting helicopter and escaped into the Appalachian Mountains, where he ate Homer slowly and with relish at the thought of his victory. He was never caught.

THE GALLANT TAILOR

Real Theme: Overachievement

It was 1979 when the bright, energetic, and popular Dwayne Curtis began to make it big in real estate. All during his boyhood he had wanted to be in apparel, either design or production, it didn't matter, but once grown up he knew he would have to do something more manly to gain any respect in the Western Hemisphere: being a tailor had decidedly effeminate connotations, and in Tucson, Arizona, a connotation was enough to ensure ridicule and failure in every aspect of life.

Tucson was modernizing, expanding, and building, so Dwayne studied, took his test, and got his license to sell real estate in 1977. Then he spent two lean years getting started with Southwest Realtors, Inc. He worked mainly on rentals, or if he sold anything, it was residences, usually the cheap ones for first time buyers. It was a stage in the business where the weak don't make it, either the buyers who go into foreclosure or the agents who have to make a career change. But Dwayne was no loser. He worked seven days a week, sixteen hours a day, and though he had to ask his father for money the first year to survive, by 1979 Dwayne was self-supporting and enjoying an increasingly wide reputation as the man to go to in Tucson.

In January he made the tremendous deal with a developer that gave him his famous nickname. He sold an empty corner of deserc first to a builder, then in March he found a group of investors to back the project while the building was still in progress. He was already in the million dollar club. The builder was putting in seven retail outlets: a laundromat, a bike store, a quick stop, a pool supply store, an auto parts store, a pizza joint, and a carpet and linoleum store. Once this deal went through, Dwayne was called "Seven At One Blow," since he had found one investor group to cover the entire shopping center, rather than just leasing or selling the businesses one by one, which would have been more time-consuming and more complicated with paperwork and licenses.

For this accomplishment Dwayne's broker, Cornell Marks, had a personalized license plate made for Dwayne's Plymouth that read, "Seven At One Blow."

It had been a stressful and backbreaking effort, though, with a lot of running around among city and county and state offices, and phoning banks and loan offices. He'd even had a date or two with an officer at the title company they used. By June, Dwayne was desperately in need of a vacation. He hadn't had any time off in over two years. So he decided to tell Cornell that he wanted a couple of weeks. Cornell was a real estate giant in southern Arizona, to set the record straight, and his size, which was medium, had nothing whatsoever to do with the designation. Many Tucson residents just referred to him as "The Giant" since he had been so instrumental in helping the area to develop.

Dwayne entered Cornell's office through the door, which had a glass window in it. He waited until Cornell was through signing a few papers on his desk. "I hope you understand that

I'm not shirking my goals, or anything, but I really need some rest." Dwayne hoped his own pale complexion, in contrast with Cornell's darkly tanned face topped by clean silver hair, would be an obvious proof of the need for such a request.

The Giant, a sporting man, who got his tan on the golf course and at the many stadia in the area, quickly jumped to his feet and said, "O.K. But only on one condition."

Apprehensive, and feeling sweat dripping down his back, his front, and his legs, in spite of the excellent air conditioning, Dwayne replied, "What's that?"

"On the condition that you engage in a series of competitions with me. If you win, you get the time off, and if I win, you don't. It's as simple as that."

Dwayne thought this was an odd way to make a decision, but brokers are known to be unconventional, or, as they call it, creative. And it was a typical masculine way to deal with an issue. He pulled his hands out of his pants pockets and said, "All right. When do we do it?"

Cornell's bright dentures showed his delight. "Right now. First, we'll have the stone squeezing."

While Dwayne looked on in confusion, Cornell reached behind his desk and came up with a large rock, which he squeezed and squeezed until water actually came out of it, as though it had been a mere dishrag. Cornell again smiled widely and his eyes twinkled in Dwayne's direction. "Now it's your turn."

Dwayne searched all through his own desk in the outer office for something even remotely resembling a stone, but all he came up with was a large round of gouda cheese he had planned to take home that night. With Cornell literally hanging over his shoulder, he squeezed this cheese, at first with trepidation, but his hand went right through it, and even more liquid came out of it than from Cornell's stone.

"How's that?" said Dwayne.

"Hmmm," said Cornell. "Looks like you win that event. But now we have the throwing contest."

Now Cornell took his wrung-out rock, what was left of it, and walked outside. He threw it up in the air as far as he could, grunting as he heaved.

Dwayne's cheese was now unserviceable, so he took the parakeet from its cage on the secretary's desk and threw that, and of course, it flew away. He looked over to Cornell to see if this was going to count.

"You've got this creative thing down pat, don't you?" said Cornell.

Next was the log carrying, and true to the facts of the previously accepted version of this story, Dwayne outsmarted the Giant by letting him carry the heavier end of a log, which Cornell kept in a storage shed in back of the office just for such contests. Since Cornell was in front, facing forward, Dwayne could, not exactly ride on the leafy end, but lean on it to conserve his energy.

Then Dwayne broke off the leafy end of the log, which was fairly straight, and after he stripped it he could use it as a pole to vault over a saguaro cactus. Because he'd been a track star in high school, this was easy for him, but Cornell didn't even try it, saying at his age his bones were too brittle to risk a vault.

"Well, it looks like you win," said Cornell but still with a friendly grin to prove he was gracious even in defeat. "But before you leave I need you to come with me to the broker's meeting of the Real Estate Council. Someone as bright and resourceful as you should be groomed for better things."

Dwayne went along with Cornell, but all morning the meeting consisted of the brokers all nagging about each other's agents and then complaining about government regulations preventing them from doing what would really be good for the industry. After that they had a session of complaining about the Indians—how they owned too much of the land. Dwayne sat next to a thin, quiet, blond, youngish-looking man, who might have been just another agent being groomed, and although neither of them said a word, they went through numerous cups of coffee during the morning, filling an entire green metal waste basket with styrofoam cups.

They broke for lunch at eleven-twenty, and all walked over to Rudy's across the street for a meal. When they started ordering martinis by the pitcher, Dwayne decided it was time to leave. He was so edgy from the coffee he didn't dare add an alcohol blur to his perceptions.

"I've got to get on my way," he whispered to Cornell.

"You can't go," hissed back Cornell, the terror in his voice sharp but pleading. "Right in front of everyone; you just can't walk out on me. I'll look like a fool. They'll never let me forget it. It'll kill my reputation."

Dwayne stood considering for a moment. The restaurant was dark and cool. "Too bad," he said.

Silence took over. All the other Giants were awed by this attitude. So independent. So powerful. So manipulative. They all privately made plans to themselves to try to get Dwayne to work for them.

He drove home to pack a suitcase; then he drove north just to relax and put some distance between Tucson and himself. Then, as he began to unwind, he started to take notice of the beautiful scenery around him. The fascinating way the saguaros grew in abundance and then at a certain height suddenly disappeared refreshed his awe of nature. He drove north on Highway 77 through Globe and Holbrook to Interstate 40 going east so he wouldn't have the big trucks slowing him up on the hills and tailgating him menacingly on the downslopes. But traffic was heavy on the interstate, and, hoping to escape crowds, he got off at State 63 going north.

106

There were a few stands on the side of the road where the Indians displayed and sold their crafts and jewelry. He was especially delighted by the hand-woven rugs and the hand-sewn shirts and dresses. He was, after all, a tailor at heart. He wished he had the courage to follow his inclinations and go into the garment industry. It was a terrible thing to be a man in America.

While he was driving he had the sense of being at home for the first time in years, and he didn't want to stop. Unfortunately he almost fell asleep at the wheel, so he had to pull over to the side of the road to sleep for a while. It was now the middle of the night and he was somewhere in the northeast corner of Arizona, but as if in some other country, some other land. He was also completely and totally lost.

When he woke up it was just sunrise, and he began to drive again. He drove and drove for miles, and the paved road became gravel, then dirt. He was in the middle of the Navajo reservation, so when he came to an Indian village, he was so relieved that in his exhaustion he just stopped where he was, turned off the motor, and fell into a deep sleep.

The Indians immediately began to walk around his car, curious because it wasn't a four-wheel drive. They wondered how he had made it this far on the rough roads without getting a flat tire or poking a hole in his gas tank and running dry in the middle of the desert. When they read the personalized license plate Cornell had given Dwayne that said, "Seven At One Blow" they were even more confused. Who was this white man? Seven what? What blow? They went to the chief of the village and reported their findings.

"He's asleep at his wheel," said a young man with short hair.

"And it's only a Plymouth," said an older, longer-haired man.

"His license plate says, 'Seven At One Blow,'" said a third.

"He must be rich," piped in a fourth.

"Wait a minute, everyone," said the chief. "It's typical of the white men to brag about something trivial. Wait until you find out. It could be as little as seven flies at one blow." Many snorts of laughter came from the men gathered around. "Let him sleep; then let's ask him the truth."

The rest of them agreed to wait, and when Dwayne woke up, he found himself being escorted to a small, wood-frame house where several women served him up a plate of stew and a cup of some kind of tasty but unidentifiable liquid.

Dwayne looked up into the round, friendly face of the chief, whose shoulder-length hair was graying. "Jackrabbit," said the chief. "We're glad to have guests." His warm brown eyes made Dwayne feel at home. "The Navajo adjust to things more easily than other Indians, you know. We came here just about the same time as you, so we've had to learn to adapt."

Dwayne dipped some brown bread in the stew. "Jackrabbit, eh?" he said. "It's delicious."

The chief smiled happily. "It's freshly caught. I sent one of my sons out to hunt while you were asleep."

Dwayne sipped from his cup. "Well, this is awfully nice of you. I feel like a bit of an intruder on your land here. I got lost."

"Nonsense," said the chief. "I'm only glad you didn't end up on Hopi land."

"Why's that?"

"Oh, well, half the time we're feuding with them, half the time we're sharing with them. It's always been that way. Right now we're feuding with them."

"Oh," said Dwayne, as the women took his empty dishes from him. "Well, I must say I like your crafts enough to be glad I didn't end up anywhere else. The weaving is exquisite."

"You like it?"

"Oh, yes. I love anything that has to do with threads, and needlework, and clothes. I always wanted to be a tailor, myself.

It's such a satisfying thing to take raw fiber, or even just a piece of cloth, and make something out of it with your own hands that's useful to wear, or I guess in the case of rugs, to walk on."

"Most people hang them up," said the chief, but not condescendingly, just informatively. "You know, I've been trying to get the men of the village to feel the way you do about weaving and sewing. They think of it as women's work. Never mind that the Pueblo men weave and most of us have Pueblo blood in our veins. My men say, 'You want us to be like them?' when I bring up the comparison. It's just a silly prejudice. There are many good things about the Pueblos."

"Sounds a lot like my world."

The chief was so touched by Dwayne's honesty and unrootedness that he offered his oldest daughter to him as a wife. This sent flashfloods of envy and resentment through the rest of the tribesmen, who knew that she carried a dowry of three fine horses and a wood-frame house. "First he must prove himself," they insisted.

Dwayne sighed. "Not again. Well, how shall it be this time?" He was again ambitious to make a success of this new opportunity, if only to refer to his competence and ability when he gave it up to follow his heart's desire some day.

The representative of the dissenters, a lawyer in clothes more appropriate to a shopping mall than to an Indian reservation, said, "We want to test your loyalty to us. Two real estate brokers are trying to buy fifty acres of land on the corner of the Reservation near Flagstaff, right near the interstate. They want to exploit it and make it a suburb of cheaply made, single-family dwellings."

Dwayne stood up to go. "And you want me to dissuade them and protect your right to the land."

"Not at all. We want you to write the contract. Get ten times what they're offering and preserve the mineral rights. Throw in a contingency that we get fifty acres of Hopi land in compensation from the government."

"You got it," said Dwayne. "And I'll just protect your rights and benefit your reputation as a little bonus." Off he drove. He was utterly confident. His nickname was "Seven At One Blow"—a little land deal was nothing for him.

The two brokers in question had offices across the street from each other, and when Dwayne drove up he made a big show of walking back and forth between the offices and of talking to all the agents about non-reservation land outside the national forest that was suitable for development. He talked about water, power, housing tracts, and title until the rumors took over in both offices. Soon the two brokers were in a bidding war and Dwayne had his way with them; they were willing to sign anything to get the Navajo land.

"Amazing," said the Navajo lawyer, when Dwayne brought back the signed contract. "And they threw in a deed for ten acres north of Winslow as a token of good faith."

"It was nothing," said Dwayne. "Now, what else can I do for you?"

"Well, now that you're at it," said another of the spokesmen, this one in more customary tribal dress of Levis and a turquoise velvet shirt, "How about proving your riding ability by capturing a herd of mustangs that have been running around the northern plateau."

Dwayne accomplished this task just as easily by finding three mares in heat from the horses around the village and by trailering them to the northern plateau, tying them together and riding the middle one seductively in front of the mustang stallion, and then leading the herd into a rope holding-pen near the village, where the Indians could take their pick.

When he got back to the village, the dissenting tribesmen and the chief were sitting around smoking and thinking up a

110

new task: the next one was to go capture a killer puma who had been raiding the sheep flocks. But Dwayne had been thinking all the way back from the plateau with the herd of mustangs. He came to the conclusion he must refuse to accept any more trivial and meaningless jobs merely to prove himself to some arbitrary self-chosen judge. He'd had enough of being tried, tested, and not accepted as adequate as he was. Having discovered the state highway on his way back with the mustangs, he respectfully took his leave of the chief's daughter and the rest of the tribe. He drove off, knowing that it was only on the open road he'd ever have a home of his own.

JACK AND THE BEANSTALK

Real Theme: Amorality

The real name of this fairy tale in the modern and factual retelling should be "Jack and the Grapevine," because in reality Jack had to drive to and from Los Angeles on the Grapevine, the part of Interstate Highway 5 that goes over the Tehachapi Mountains, in order to get his bag of gold, his gold-egg-laying hen, and his singing harp. Jack lived in Bakersfield, the most southerly city in the Central Valley of California. Many people think the Tehachapis are the most natural boundary between Northern and Southern California.

Mabel Davis, Jack's mother, was the leader of the group most concerned with that issue: the California Secession Movement. The CSM was a growing group of people from throughout the state, and they planned to have California secede from the United States on the basis that California has one of the top five Gross National Products among all nations of the world, and because the other states tend to show disrespect and even abuse towards California as a mecca of immorality, the CSM believes they should try supporting themselves on their own taxes. The amount Californians pay in Federal Income Tax would be better used solving their own state's rather trivial problems, one main one being the constant immigration from other states.

Mabel was a vigorous, thin woman of forty-five with graying hair and an ebullient manner. She was an electrifying and charismatic public speaker and she signed up new supporters in droves every time she lectured on CSM or related topics. She argued that the only other historical secession, that of the Confederate States of America, or "The South," had the serious flaw that Southerners are by nature chauvinistic, militaristic, and antagonistic to everyone else; naturally they rose to the challenge to fight when invaded; they even provoked the war. Mabel suggested a plan for the California secession: if the US Army invades, as they must to keep their treasury from being forever empty, Californians should counter by inviting the soldiers into their hot tubs, offering them glasses of wine, and encouraging them to talk about their early childhood, their repressed feelings about their spouses, bosses, or officers, or about their sex lives and the sources of their feelings of hostility and aggression.

Mabel's problem, as with most non-profit groups, was funding. Even with an active mail solicitation campaign, the CSM was constantly in desperate need of funds. There was an entire wing of the movement dedicated to solving the problems between Northern and Southern California, primarily water usage and air pollution standards, and this meant money was needed for travelling, lobbying in Sacramento, publishing the controversies in pamphlets and brochures, and holding public debates with question and answer periods.

The Davises were, of course, Californians from the beginning: the 1850's. Bakersfield to this day retains its 1950's charm, with its styles of signs, buildings, bowling alleys, drive-ins, and its Greyhound Bus Station, but despite four generations, Mabel did not have much local wealth to count on either from family or from friends and neighbors. So she sent Jack to LA to try to stir up some backing; he was to promise that new water projects would be the first order of business once we got the federal government off our backs.

Jack was a rather slow young man, never a go-getter and actually complacent at times, preferring to live with his parents rather than join the Army, go to college, or get a job like most normal young people. He also was on the thin side and a chain smoker, but he was not unattractive to women. However, he was socially clumsy, and one or two dates with a woman was all it generally took for her to think of some excuse not to go out with him again.

Like most American men, Jack had an unusual fixation on his mother, something it is to be suspected that was either an unresolved Oedipal conflict from some crisis that took place in the family during his adolescence or something that was the result of the way most American men treat their women. Jack's father, though technically still alive, contrary to reports in earlier versions of the tale, was so consumed with his own career as an irrigation equipment salesman and socializing with his contacts in the business that he never had time for Mabel and Jack.

This explains why, when Mabel told Jack to go to LA to solicit funds for the CSM, he obeyed unquestioningly. He had no reason to be rebellious.

Jack took the three magic beans (three tabs of benzedrine). He did have a slight dependence on certain recreational drugs, though he never took hallucinogenic drugs because he found reality bizarre enough. He needed a little stimulation to keep up with it. He jumped into his Toyota and drove over the Grapevine into LA on a cool clear morning in February.

On the freeway once he was in the city, he decided to try his one connection in the entertainment industry, video recording mogul Bob Hansen, who had made his fortune producing rock albums and now financed not just video promos and cassettes, but movies and TV series as well. Jack and the band he played in, "The Rainbirds," had auditioned for Bob years ago, and though Bob probably wouldn't remember it with all he had on his mind these days, Jack knew he could get in the door of the Bel-Air mansion if he mentioned the fact that Bob had told him to come back for another audition if he ever thought up any original material.

Bob was out by the pool in his bathrobe, sitting in a deck chair and drinking coffee when the housekeeper let Jack in. The housekeeper was oblivious, no doubt new to the West Coast, a matronly woman of fifty, who didn't ask any questions, listened to Jack's speech, and disappeared as soon as she had gestured Jack towards the back door, saying with no noticeable accent, "He's sitting out there admiring the view."

Jack was glad to be left alone and he wanted to watch Bob secretly for a few minutes—since the entertainment giant was usually surrounded by young blonde blue-eyed sexpots—but a dissonant sight prevented any spying. On the mantle above the unused brick fireplace Jack's eye was caught by what appeared to be a bag of gold. He sneaked over to it: it was a small burlap sack with Krugerrands and Maple Leafs spilling out the top. Jack took no time at all to stuff the overflow back in the sack and quietly walk out with it. It was really too easy, but soon he was speeding over the Grapevine with a bag of gold for the moment worth hundreds of thousands. No one but the mindless house-keeper had even known he was there, and she would never be able to identify him.

The part of the story about the giant saying "Fee, fie, foe, fum, I smell the blood of an Englishman," was obviously put in by the 19th century British fairy tale compilers, with their

115

passion for nonsense syllables, rhymes of any quality, and the persecution complexes that come as the result of an island existence.

Actually Jack couldn't hear anything being said outside because the sliding glass door to the patio was closed. He assumed Bob was making passes at the blondes or bragging about his yacht or new helicopter.

Mabel was delighted when he returned home so successful. She deposited all the gold in market rate accounts, once she had converted it into more liquid cash, a hundred thousand in each bank, since that was all that was federally insured. "That's one change we'll make immediately," she thought; it would have been nice to keep it all in one place with the same high interest. "When California is its own nation, the money market accounts will be insured to any amount."

So, the CSM was funded for months and made noteworthy expansions both in membership and mailing list.

All was going well when there was a budget crisis in Sacramento. Mabel was opportunistic enough to know the benefits of hiring laid-off state workers to stuff envelopes, make phone calls, and ring doorbells for the CSM, but this depleted her own funds so much that she had to rouse Jack from his large pillow in front of the television, where he was watching Mayberry RFD on the local channel that played all the old 1950's and '60's series every afternoon.

"You'll have to go back to LA and get me some more money. Gold was fine but cash, stocks and bonds—even investment gems—will do just as well," she told him.

Feeling a momentary pang of guilt, Jack said, "Don't you even want to know where I got it?"

"No," said his mother. "Some causes are so important they transcend morality."

"How do you know I got it in an immoral way?" he asked, not ready to get up from his comfortable pillow.

She smiled, "Long years of life on earth. Now stop stalling and give up Burns and Allen for one day."

Jack climbed into the Toyota, wishing it had air conditioning because the temperature was 95° that August afternoon. He drove over the Grapevine and into the thick brown haze of a second-stage smog alert.

There was a new housekeeper at Bob's. Jack realized the other one probably got blamed for the missing bag of gold. Nevertheless, he went through the same story as before. This new housekeeper was a pale woman in her thirties with dark circles under her eyes as though she had eight children to bring up on her own, but with an imperious and suspicious attitude as though she had something on Bob. Still, she let Jack in and said she would call Bob down. He was upstairs watching some new rock and roll videos that he had financed but not actually made decisions about.

Once she was gone Jack knew he had several minutes alone, so he quickly and cautiously rummaged through the downstairs rooms. In the formal dining room, on a long walnut table covered in a handmade lace tablecloth, he found an ordinary barnyard hen sitting on a purple velvet pillow, on a solid gold egg, as though she were trying to hatch it. Jack somehow had known something would be there. Jack took the hen and the velvet pillow and rushed out of the mansion. He drove back home over the Grapevine. This hen proved to lay a golden egg every day, and if his mother spent moderately she knew she could always count on new money from the sale of the eight to ten ounces of top quality gold.

Thinking that now he could vegetate in peace the rest of his days in front of the TV, Jack forgot all about his two burglaries. But Mabel was still not content. A month or two later she said, "You know, we're so close to secession; we just need something to push us over the top, to solidify North and South into agreeing on a vote to declare independence."

117

Jack didn't need a more direct hint. He obediently got up, turned off Green Acres, and jumped into his car and drove the familiar route to Bob's house. A man answered the door this time and in an English accent said he would announce Jack to Bob, who was in his den talking on the telephone to Japan.

The singing harp was sitting on the grand piano in the living room humming "Open Arms" quietly to itself. Jack recognized its uniqueness and importance and assumed that, led by a singing harp, the state would quickly unify and "California, Here I Come", or "Stoned in Love" would easily replace the long and loathsome "Star Spangled Banner" as the new national anthem for the new nation. Certainly this was exactly what his mother wanted.

Jack began to sneak out with the harp in his arms when Bob came out of the den, hand extended as though to shake hands with Jack. Jack raced out the front door and jumped into his Toyota and sped off. By the time Bob in his Mercedes caught him they were going over the Grapevine. Jack easily pushed Bob off the freeway and down the side of the mountain. Bob was killed instantly. Unfortunately, the singing harp had truly loved Bob and never sang again because of its grief, so the CSM had to struggle on in doubt and factionalism.

Research may make other versions of this tale surface, such as the one where the giant's wife helps Jack to hide, but Bob Hansen was never married and never had even one steady girlfriend. This is the true story: all the others are frauds.

SNOW WHITE

Real Theme: Anguish

A mere typographical error is responsible for the current misconceptions about the Snow White story. It has previously been believed that the chant addressed to the magic mirror on the wall was "Mirror, mirror, on the wall, who is the fairest one of all?" This mistake has come down through history and influenced all interpretations of the meaning of the fairy tale. Actually the chant should have been and should be "Mirror, mirror, on the wall, who is the free-est one of all?" It's easy to understand the confusion with all those e's, but that's no excuse to continue the error.

Snow White was not the standard cliché of fairy tales as certain compilers would have us believe; she was not a princess, but, in fact, an actress, twenty-seven years old, and quite talented. She had turned down several offers, against the advice of her agent, for TV series and movies, and opted instead for the theater, spending most summers in Ashland, Oregon, acting in the plays of the Shakespeare Festival. Her agent, Roberta Walsh, who was libelously called the evil stepmother in the watered-down 19th century version, was a failed actress herself, *was* jealous of Snow, and *was* trying to kill her by working her to death, but she was never even a surrogate mother, much less surrogate evil stepmother.

The important thing about the story, though, is not the violent—actually B-grade—horror movie plot, but instead the fact that Snow had an exaggerated, therefore exemplary, sense of the existential phenomenon of anguish. Along with that was her anger and bitterness, called penis envy by the crass, over the fact that she had always wanted to play the part of Hamlet.

Snow didn't get along well with other women, something that should have tipped her off about Roberta at the beginning. But having a male agent wasn't the solution, either. How could she be sure a man would be sensitive to her artistic needs and get the necessary parts to advance her career without sacrificing integrity and her own high standards of good taste?

Anyway, in the summer of 1978, Snow answered an ad in the Medford Gazette for a room to rent, and when she discovered she would have seven male roommates, she was delighted not to have to put up with any nit-picky, bitchy, gossipy, back-stabbing females. Traditionally we heard that these seven were dwarves who spent the day in mines digging for gold. In fact, these seven men were all unattached and had to spend their time trying to avoid being caught by gold diggers of the other gender.

Though authentic versions of this story do not name these seven at all, one twentieth century source not only calls them dwarves but gives them cutesy little names, demeaning them past any forgiveness. Obviously the earlier stories either neglected their names or never knew them. The gentleman in charge of the house was actually named Dennis. He was 5'7" and slender, with a heavy beard and short blackish hair—a house painter by trade. He had inherited the old country house, located in a stunning little valley several miles outside Medford on the Ashland side, from his grandmother, and, after repairs and of course a fresh coat of paint, he converted the lower rooms to bedrooms so the house could keep eight easily, then he began advertising for roommates. This way he had a regular monthly expectation of money to augment the erratic income he made seasonally at painting.

On the second level in the five bedrooms upstairs were Jeff, the car salesman; Bill, a short-order cook; Alan, an electrician; Milt, an unemployed factory worker; and Brad, a college student supported by Federally Insured Student Loans. They were all over 5'6", so the dwarf rumor was only an anti-male slur.

The seventh roommate, Lance, who had the back bedroom on the ground floor, was also an actor in the Shakespeare Festival. It was his first year at it, and he often kept Snow up half the night asking questions and talking shop. There was no suspicion of an affair with Lance, though, because he was gay. He secretly had a thing for Bill but hid it well since all the others were straight and he didn't want to offend them. They did like Lance, and if they teased him it was not malicious, but in fun, the way they teased each other about their own peccadilloes and idiosyncrasies.

Dennis put Snow White in the bedroom across the hall from his, "to keep her safe from these animals." Hers was a converted parlor and his a converted dining room. The large country kitchen they all used in common because the other ground floor sitting room was Lance's converted bedroom. This meant there were considerable crossings of thresholds to borrow deodorant, toothpaste, aspirin, and the like. After Snow discouraged Lance from the late-night acting seminars, she became attracted to Milt, who, after all, was always there.

She began to visit his room and soon the entire house knew what was going on. They accepted it as a natural thing at once. There were no eyebrows raised, no subtle condemnatory airs or comments. Milt was blond and through weight-lifting had built himself up to a hundred and eighty-five pounds of solid muscle. Snow, though she had very white skin, black hair, and red lips, just like we were always told, was attracted to blond men: they seemed so vulnerable.

The affair went on with Milt for a couple of months while Snow was playing Desdemona, a part she detested, and Imogen, a part she only mildly disliked. Shakespeare's women, like everything about Shakespeare, had been studied and discussed to death by all levels of competent and incompetent critics, and Snow figured that bringing life to Cordelia, Rosalind, Portia, Ophelia, or any of the other ludicrously named characters was about all anyone could ask for.

Anyway, after the first two passionate months, Milt began to expect her to cook and clean up while he read cheap Westerns, and she soon got bored with him and stopped going into his room. Under Dennis' watchful and just barely uncondemning eye, she began taking up with Jeff, a more ambitious person entirely, with the glib manner a car salesman must have. He was also meticulous and a good cook, and he was undemanding though not blond, so Snow didn't have to fit into the standard sex roles, which of all parts on earth to play she found the most impossible.

The biggest drawback was that Jeff was functionally illiterate and said he could never make a word of sense of Shakespeare in a book, a movie, or on TV, and he couldn't really see the point of plays or stories anyway. Though never an intellectual snob or bigot, Snow soon found Jeff's limits and longed for more from a relationship, though she was discreet enough not to show it so as not to hurt his feelings.

Dennis should have been able to foretell this, but he had fallen in love with Snow at first sight, and that had precluded normal reasoning. Before the season was over Snow had gone through all the roommates. He didn't know that this was a symptom of her anguish; he was simply himself heartbroken and anguished in the dictionary sense. Fortunately no one had anything contagious, so the promiscuity didn't cost anybody a germless body. Dennis was sullen and he avoided Snow. He had expected her to sense his feeling and reciprocate. Though he didn't demand virginity in these sexually liberated times, a fair measure of modesty wasn't too much to ask, in his opinion. He was the only one of the seven she hadn't gone through yet, so as winter came on, she started to put the make on him and was naturally bewildered by his rebuffs and refusals.

Meanwhile Roberta was trying to get work for Snow in movies: a part as a corset stay saleswoman at the turn of the century in the surrealistic semi-biographical movie of the life of Sarah Bernhardt, a part Snow refused outright as too sexist in perspective; and a virtually assured part as a hairstylist in the second year of the hit TV series "Comb-Out," but Snow refused that because she thought it was too tacky.

Not surprisingly, this began to get on Roberta's nerves. She went to the magic mirror and asked "Mirror, mirror, on the wall, who is the free-est one of all?" when the mirror replied, "Walsh, thou art of freedom rare, but Snow White living there in sin, with all those seven horny men, is the free-est one of all." Roberta, who hadn't indulged her own lust since that pick-up at the Lumber Room in downtown Medford, was understandably a bit envious.

Snow, feeling truly rejected for the first time in her life, began to lose her confidence with men, and the anguish that had only polluted her soul began to poison it. It got to be more than she could stand. Now, with the season over and no acting to force her mind to focus, she started to feel a kind of inverted stage fright: a *reality* fright. Once she was in a part or on stage, she knew what the perimeters of existence and her own capacity for behavior were. If she was afraid of forgetting a line or of stumbling over a prop, that was a natural thing for actors and forgivable. It rarely happened to her, though, because she was very good.

No, the anguish wasn't caused by any threats of danger from the outside. It was the existential type of anguish, where she felt like turning to the audience—say during the last scene in Lear where she's supposed to be dead—and saying, "Cordelia is a chump; I should be doing Hamlet." Luckily her anguish was controllable up until the end of the season, so she restrained herself from committing such a career-destroying error on stage.

Now, with her mind and imagination free of acting parts in plays, she began to feel anguish; even while driving, for example, she had the desire to let go of the wheel and let destiny take its course with her only as a free and neutral observer; or at the supermarket the urge to knock over a display of canned corn that was stacked to the ceiling seemed to express the idea: our structures are infinitely fragile compared to the forces they must stand up against. It went so far that as she stood on a bridge over the Rogue River, thinking in great detail how delicious it might feel to let the river carry her along—not against her will but with her will in total harmony, a thought growing naturally out of her initial fear of what would happen if she accidentally fell in, that she narrowly missed jumping in.

Fortunately for Snow White, about that time Dennis began to forgive her for her behavior with the others. He began to court her in all the traditional ways without making any physical passes. He took her out to dinner and to a movie, he cooked them an intimate candlelight dinner after getting rid of the other six for the evening, he bought her flowers and an opal necklace, and he seriously asked if they might be engaged to be married, holding her hand in both of his at the time. This chivalry and quaintness amused Snow White, and thinking of the lost values of earlier historical periods when we weren't quite so free, she consented to be married.

So the next time Roberta went to the magic mirror and asked, "Mirror, mirror on the wall, who is the free-est one of all?" the mirror said, "Snow White's an idiot, her freedom's gone: Walsh, thou art for sure the free-est one." This made Roberta so happy she began working on a novel about show business.

Dennis threw out the boarders and fixed up the house for the two of them and any subsequent children. Snow White, who was incidentally a third or fourth cousin to Thelma White, but not on the side where the hen characteristics always surface, had four children in the next seven years, and they wore her out so that she never acted or had a life of her own again.

The traditional tale has her falling asleep and being awakened by a handsome prince, then marrying and making the step-mother dance to her death in red-hot shoes. Happy endings are for children. The harsh truth is that Snow White died at the age of sixty-two and was reincarnated as a brine shrimp.

TOM THUMB

Real Theme: Academic Excellence

Once upon a time, on October 23, 1983, Tom Thumb sat in his favorite coffeehouse, The Silver Swan, a couple of blocks from the University of Chicago. Tom was a graduate student in Economics, but since he loathed the idea of a suit and tie, a regular and substantial paycheck which would burden him with the responsibility of making all the decisions as to how it would be spent, and the dull routine of a job, he kept taking classes, one or two at a time, stalling in every way possible to keep from taking the degree to stay a student as long as he could. He lived on money from the G.I. Bill, having enlisted safely in the army in 1973. He had spent some time in Europe, but was stationed most of his active duty in Hawaii where he was a clerk to some colonel who was the coordinator of the Army-Navy interservices sports program. Tom pulled this easy duty because he was unnaturally short—less than three feet tall. In another era in history this might have precluded military service, but the Army was very hard up after all the protests against the Vietnam War, so they had to take what they could get.

Upon this time is was four in the afternoon. Tom decided to allow himself another cup of coffee. Two cups in the morning and two cups in the afternoon were his limit for the day. The song "If I Had a Hammer" had been going through his head all day. He decided that if one had to philosophize, it would be best to do it with a hammer like crazy Nietzsche. But the anachronism of the song: danger, warning, love? All over this land? He must have been thinking of this because he'd seen in the paper the advertisement for the Peter, Paul, and Mary revival concert that night. He might have considered going, since he had once enjoyed their harmonies, but the thought of the conversations about how old they looked that would be going on all around the audience made him cringe. Not only that, he thought, but Peter, Paul, and Mary had probably sold out and gone religious, like Bob Dylan.

There were two men he had never seen before in the coffeehouse, sitting next to the small stage where musicians played and poets read out loud most evenings of the week. They were playing what looked like a very absorbing game of chess. Chess was Tom's passion, barely but consistently winning out over eating. He longed to play chess at that moment himself as these two men were: it would feel so good to checkmate someone. It was not an intellectual interest, but a passionate desire in him; he was so good at chess that there was no real satisfaction except in playing ten or twelve games at a time and being able to checkmate the opponents all within several minutes of the start. He could do this at pool and ping pong as well, but those sports involved too much exercise. They made him work up so much appetite he had to eat two or three dinners, and that was dangerously fattening for one who burned fewer calories than normal because of his size.

Though Tom was small, he remained existentially sound due to his exceptionally high IQ, and he rarely suffered from anxiety, despair, or any other modern malady. He didn't have a short man's complex: he would have been scornful towards anyone who judged anyone else by such a superficial thing as size. He would suggest they look inside to find him in his true essence: a unique individual who had never set foot inside a shopping mall, who didn't even know what Tupperware was, who had never once ordered fast food—in short, someone who had rejected all the baits of this superficial and herd-oriented society.

He spent most days at the coffeehouse. He loved the discussions between graduate students that took place most of the time. That afternoon, after lusting for the chess board, Tom found himself seated nexted to Andy McKnee, a Political Science major. Andy had a job application in front of him on the rectangular brown table. The form had been given to him by a corporate recruiter on campus that morning.

Between bites of his bargain lunch of vegetable soup and bread, Andy said, "Industry and technology thrive on this kind of mass-marketing. They don't care who you really are."

Tom was considering a piece of fresh-baked carrot cake. "I would use it as a napkin, if I were you."

Andy said, "I don't even know how I got into the meeting. I thought I was going to a lecture by Alexander Haig. Instead here are these clones from the Clorox Group asking me to sell out my ideals and my self to take a job in modern commercialized big business."

Tom decided against the cake, but the self-denial was a strain. "As though we need to be demeaned and dehumanized. The decadent throngs abhor an idealist."

The beautiful but predictable Veronica Palmer, a history major, said, "We could be teachers but the tenure system in education has corrupted the teaching profession severely. Educated and intelligent people have less status in the herd mind than immigrants and ghetto dwellers. The ivory tower today is the ivory slum."

128

And so they went on, day in, day out, about individuation, differentiation, independence, and achieving a higher existence or at least a higher state of consciousness for a while. The usual song and dance about personality fragmentation and/or integration went on many afternoons in the oblique autumn rays of city light.

Tom's favorite subject to bring up was the Supreme Person, the innermost self that dwells forever in the hearts of all beings. He was fond of making the joke that in the Hindu Upanishad, Katha, the Supreme Person is no bigger than a thumb.

Another speech in Tom's repertoire was, "Greatness comes from self-denial," which he might say turning to Veronica while they sat at a table and were both relatively the same height. This line of reasoning he saved for times when she might be complaining about not having any money.

When his wife called up with the notion that he could be made to pay the child support for their son in New Mexico when Tom had seen neither of them for four years, he would tell her, "Childhood is an invention of modern times, artificial and meaningless."

Now there are several different versions of "Tom Thumb" floating around (as is usual with fairy tales because before this writing no one either knew the real story, or if they did, they tried to set it down but didn't do it properly). These outrageous lies assert that Tom did pretend to sell himself, but after receiving money from the impresarios who wanted to exploit him as a show piece, he escaped down a mouse hole; that he consorted with thieves; and the more ridiculous rumor that he was eaten by a cow. Impossible, all: Tom was a man of character, a moral man.

In the true version his actions should be represented as much less melodramatic. Seized by the impulse to get a change of scene, he strolled out of the coffeehouse and down to the campus. On the way he met Beth Shinn, the coed from Spring-

129

field who was desperately in love with him. She has no subtlety about her passions, he thought. She didn't disgust him for, in truth, he considered her a moderately intelligent and pleasantly attractive woman, but she just didn't romantically move him.

"Tom," she said in a breathy voice, catching up with him, "I've finally finished my paper on Milton. I wish you would read through it for me before I have to turn it in." She brushed a strand of short blond hair back out of her intense brown eyes.

"I have no training in English Lit.," he returned. They walked between a block of filthy and high buildings. He had a sudden wish that she weren't five eight. Not that size mattered . . .

"No, I mean just for grammar and technicalities," she said. "I'm so bad at it and you're so disciplined."

"You're the typical result of grade school after the radical sixties," he muttered. He took the paper and dismissed her with a sharp, "I'll see you later." He knew this exercise was only an excuse for her to talk to him, so with a compassionate attitude, he indulged her.

Once on campus he took an elevator up to the floor where the professors' offices were. It wasn't Rex's office hours, but Tom's mentor and sponsor, Rex Radius, might be in his office, anyway, working on his book, *The Crime of Andrew Jackson: A Return To Hard Currency.* The door to the office was closed, but Tom tried it, and the knob turned. As always when he entered his teacher's presence, Tom experienced a thrilling sensation unmatched by any other existent phenomenon.

"Am I interrupting?" Tom asked, as Rex looked up.

Rex smiled and said, "Just listen to this: 'It is mandatory we in the civilized world give up the paper money habit. The first benefit would be the improvement in the physical condition of the population, as the billfold junkies would be forced to increase their strength by carrying around large sacks of heavy gold and silver coins, if not bricks.'"

"Revolutionary," said Tom. "This could mean a Pulitzer if not a Nobel."

"I don't think it's enough," said the tall and charismatic teacher, who still had all his hair, with not a one turned gray. His smooth, lightly tanned skin was youthful and healthy looking but only enough to look good, not enough to look indulgent. "I'm afraid I'm blocked. I'm trying to argue for a referendum to bring back the hard currency standard, but I'm battling myself: let's face it, paper money is more convenient. It just debases faster."

Afraid to suggest he consider starting over with an entirely new book topic, or worse, to suggest what Tom considered inevitable, the cashless society where everything would be paid at the bank by credit or debit card, or better yet, by fingerprint, Tom said, "If you have no money at all it really doesn't matter much to you." He felt guilty that he didn't want to give away that he half considered starting a book about it himself.

"Don't give in too soon," said Rex, rubbing his unspectacled eyes, still 20-20 even though he was forty-one. "You'll just end up one more mediocrity like me, pounding out book after book no one reads except a few critics chosen by my publisher."

Tom sat down on the desk, next to the word processor. He was almost on a level with Rex now. "Sometimes I wonder," he said, unable to keep portentousness out of his tone.

Rex leaned back. "About what?"

"Well," said Tom, utilizing maximum eye contact, "I believed school was a place for learning and for intelligence, and I thought my niche in life was to be a professor, write important books, contribute to human intelligence, and discuss all the highest thoughts and theories; all that."

"Naiveté can strike at any time."

"I hated the redundancy and traditionalism of the military— not the discipline, but the meaningless and thoughtless standard practices, with no room for innovation or creativity. The business world seemed the same: it just paid better and the uniforms were less gaudy. Now it seems the university system is pretty much the same."

"Not exactly," said Rex. "Here we have three square inches of room for innovation and creativity. Not much, but it's all you're going to get and still draw a regular paycheck."

"What a terrible choice," mused Tom.

Rex interrupted: "Look, you're getting close to your degree. Soul-searching is a normal function, a rite of passage. Next year we have a couple of department retirements and I think I'll be asked to be department head."

Tom was interested. "So, I have a pretty good chance of getting on."

Rex smiled, showing his perfectly straight, perfectly white teeth. "You're the best qualified man for the job. Now you'll have to think of a book to start writing, and I'll set up a conference with my publisher for you."

"To be honest," Tom said, "I *was* thinking about a book about a cashless society. Something like, *Charge By Fingers: The Golden Touch*."

"Fine," Rex said. "There, if you're working on something positive and constructive, these dark little doubts and questions will never enter your mind. Remember, St. Augustine had doubts too."

Tom felt rejuvenated and happy as he left the office. He wondered which office would be his next year. Which books should he bring for the shelves? What wall hangings to put up? How would he dress? What lecture style would he use? How hard would he grade? His imagination soared as he took the elevator down, giving him a frightening and staggering moment of vertigo at the ground level.

He went back to the coffee house and wrote an outline for freshman classes for one year, he was so enthused. Then he began to daydream about tenure, department head, a call from Washington to request his talents as a budget consultant. He was delighted to think of the large audience he would soon have for his highly polished lectures and anecdotes.

There was another bleak moment late that afternoon when he considered the possibilities that would have been open to him had he followed his early instincts and gone into mathematics or physics, but it was only hunger. He went home to his apartment, a room over a pharmacy, and had a meal of a lamb chop and a baked potato. Braced for the night he returned to the Swan, where some madrigal singers were just finishing, and the aspiring poets were ready to begin another evening of developing resonant reading voices.

PETER RABBIT

Real Theme: Technitis

Peter Rabbit suffered from the malaise of the eighties and was one of the first post-existentialist victims of modern life who could have heartily benefitted from a little soul-strengthening dread, ennui, anxiety, or *weltschmertz*. Pete was told all the time he was growing up that computers were the entire future of mankind and all who trained themselves in the science early would be in the forefront of human endeavor all their lives.

Ambitious, confident, fascinated, Pete studied computers as a hobby, though he actually majored in political science. His interest in the world waned when he reached maturity and, as he hit his prime he was a full-blown sufferer of man's most extreme self-imposed wound: technitis. Yes, Pete bought everything we all heard in those days: children would be able to learn through computers—thus a revolution in education; businesses could be made infinitely more prosperous through computers—thus a revolution in economics; space exploration was tied intimately to computers and was the salvation of a rather slovenly and destructive mankind, who if it didn't blow itself to bits, would pollute the planet into being uninhabitable—thus a revolution on a universal scale.

Pete worked as a computer salesman for IBM all during the seventies, when only large corporations were interested in this magic tool, this mechanical messiah. Then, to his infinite satisfaction, the small computer craze either hit or was imposed on society (depending on your point of view). Pete was involved in several ill-conceived and badly managed small companies and then found a home teaching classes to the converted hoards on the use of personal computers.

Of course he could throw around the language better than anyone: peripherals, bytes, software, bits, floppy disk, and so on; he could buzzword circles around any ordinary citizen. He spent his spare time reading science fiction books, which he had fallen in love with in high school. He dreamed of the day man and perhaps he himself would propel humanity up into space on an orbiting colony on a space station, or on the moon, or on another planet. Like all the masses of techies in the world, he completely lost his perspective, and in trying to keep himself in the lead of the race for superiority in artificial intelligence, alas, he completely neglected to develop any concept or sense of reality for the word wisdom, and, some thought, quite cruelly overlooked the whole picture of existence in the universe for a few beautiful but limited views.

Pete had grown up in the outskirts of Baltimore and had three unsuccessful marriages, but they really can't be blamed on his technitis. One was a high school romance outgrown, as most first marriages are. Another was an on-the-rebound error. The third was ongoing, and verged on successful, but Pete was married to his machines and his visions of epic greatness as pictured on a TV screen in green letters.

He and his third wife, Mahalia, had moved to Washington, D.C., where Pete could indulge both his habit and his hobby at the same time. They lived in a pleasant little neighborhood, not far from the elite wealthy neighborhoods of the politicians but a healthy distance from the slums. Mahalia, a secretary, was a beautiful and vivacious blonde woman, who kept her own last name of Nichols upon marriage rather than take the last name of Rabbit, which she thought fine for popular singers or truck-drivers.

Pete taught nights at the city college and brought the new world into people's minds each quarter at a pretty low wage, he thought, but he loved doing it, so that was worth something. His tall blond charismatic head faced the classroom full of the frightened but determined faces of those who had been convinced they were doomed without a tie-in to reality in the form of computerese, if not in the form of their own microcomputer.

Soon, though, something began to cloy in Pete. For some reason he wasn't enjoying himself. He felt a desire, a yearning, a hunger for something more. One night in their cute little three bedroom house, after the vegetarian dinner Mahalia cooked, Pete lingered at the table, elbows up on it, staring at his plate, empty but for the three pieces of string bean too tough to chew.

"I'm going to have to find something else," he said. "I love teaching, but it's just getting to be too much of a drain on me. I have to spend so much time repeating the same things over and over."

I'm not surprised to hear you say it," returned Mahalia. "It has been taking up too much of your time. We never get away for the weekend any more. We hardly have time for anything else."

Mahalia was herself in a crisis over her job: she had been at the same desk and typewriter for two years, a long enough time to spend in one place. But the two men whose work she typed up and whose coffee she made were anachronisms, holdovers from the fifties and sixties, who both assumed she was going to be there for the rest of her life and who never failed to be shocked by her salty language.

"I have to find something that is a little less draining," he said with a sigh.

"Well, it's time for a change, then, isn't it?" She got up but didn't take the plates because they had the arrangement that if one of them cooked the dinner the other one had to clean up.

"I'm getting so tired of changing jobs, though," he said, pushing the half-chewed beans around his plate.

"Why? Just think of it as a matter of interchangeable parts. Think of yourself as a custom integrated circuit." When she was in a cheerful mood her voice had the quality of chimes.

"Yes," Pete agreed, brightening, "a custom integrated circuit whose career is trending in the direction of a change of scenery."

"That's right." Mahalia had been holding herself up by hanging on to a chair back, but now she yawned and stretched. "Well," she said, "it's time to interface with a bathtub for me."

Pete smiled up at her and reached to squeeze her shoulder as she walked by. She had such a way of propping him up.

After he had loaded the dishwasher, he called to Mahalia, "I'll see you after class," and left the house. He drove to the school and parked his car. He had a *Washington Post* in the back seat he'd been saving to read before class over a cup of coffee. As usual, he flipped right through the front page section with its obsessive concern with politics and depressing world news. He read the movie and book reviews, the business page to look for inspiration for his program on picking stock market winners, and then spent most of the time on the sports page.

He left the paper in the cafeteria after he'd finished his coffee and then he wandered to his classroom. His computers were

137

sitting and waiting for him like well-behaved dogs, tied up and wanting him to come walk them. This was truly where the magic occurred. Even if the industry was changing so quickly that it took all his time to keep up with the latest designs and capacities, at least he could make a class full of people familiar with the basics of the state of the art. Many were simply intimidated by the unknown. Many had to be told that in most ordinary cases it's not necessary to have thousands of dollars worth of equipment.

He walked around the room, switching all the machines to "ON" and letting the electric power begin to flow into all the dead plastic and metal, giving it life. Then suddenly, there was a thunderous explosion not far away, so that the room rocked and the window glass shook. Pete, like everyone, ran outside and followed several young women students out to the street.

The explosion had started a fire in a government building down the street, and the orange flames were already blazing upwards above the roof.

"Was it a bomb or something?" asked one of the students, hugging her books to her chest.

Self-conscious of his large ears, which he tried to cover by wearing his hair slightly longer than most techies, Pete said, "It could have been natural gas . . . a leak in a pipe, ignited by a lit match."

The girls looked at him strangely and laughed to each other, leaning together.

"Or, it could have been a bomb," he conceded.

He watched for a few minutes and then returned to his classroom, thankful the disaster hadn't caused a power black-out. He began to hear the sirens of the fire department, police, and ambulances scream toward him from different directions. The smell of the smoke was heavy on the air.

He looked at the clock. 7:15. Not one of his students had arrived. Out with the crowds, watching the fire, no doubt. Voyeurs, he thought bitterly.

When another quarter hour went by without anyone showing up, he began to play with his computers. He had several assignments he'd been hired for by private businesses. One was to write a program for the storage of different sized boxes for a toy distributor, and another was for the replacement of parts for a large chain muffler shop. If not that, he could work on his stock market program or his football game prediction program. There was always something for him to do, if not fill his wallet with these outside jobs and projects, then work on a new design for a computer game. If he could invent one that would be as popular as Pac-Man or Burgertime, his fortunes would be made and he'd never have to hold a job again.

Time escaped Pete. Maybe a student or two had come to the open door, looked in to see no one there, and left. Maybe they were afraid of the fire spreading. The janitor finally had to throw him out at midnight. Sirens had been heard in the streets all night, and the fire was still going strong when he walked out of the school. By now, though, the crowds were thinner. He saw one of his students, a mother of four named Bonnie Wyatt, and he joined her behind the police barricade.

"Isn't it awful?" she said once she saw him. They watched firemen chopping at the roof and the walls that remained and shooting great streams of water into the smoky flames. An ambulance sat waiting just behind the fire trucks.

"Have many people been injured?" asked Pete.

"I got here a little late, so I'm not sure. They must have gotten most of them out quickly, or else the building was empty." Bonnie smiled. "I couldn't think of coming to class with all this going on outside."

"You weren't alone." Pete smiled back into her eyes. "We'll have to consider it a cancelled class. No punishment." He wanted to tell her how much everyone missed and how the course would be thrown off now, but he felt she wouldn't understand.

"It's just awful," she said again, turning to the fire, but with a look of fascination. Her cheeks were flushed, and her lips were parted.

Pete resisted his impulse to stare at her. "Did they find out what caused it?" he asked.

"Some people who were here earlier said it was a terrorist bomb. But what bizarre group would want to blow up government surplus canned goods?"

"Is that what they had in there? I always figured it was TV's and stereos."

"No. I suppose there's some reasoning behind it. Maybe some group representing the poor, who didn't want that stuff distributed to make the Republicans look generous and get reelected."

Pete looked at her again and thought, what a nut. He stayed a few more minutes then took his leave and started to drive home.

Three blocks from home he witnessed a hit-and-run accident. But just as he approached the disabled car, he suddenly figured out a step on his toy storage program which had stumped him for days. Knowing someone else would be along any minute, he hurried to his house to write down his inspiration. Soon he would make enough money to buy his own computer equipment so he could work at home without bringing components from the school.

Mahalia was up, reading in bed. Pete changed into his pajamas and jumped on his side of the bed, under the covers. On his bedside table were his copies of "Impact" and "On-Line" for the month, and he reached for them to flip through before sleeping.

Mahalia said, "I've been thinking."

"Oh."

"Yes. I think it's my turn for a job change. If I have to work another month with those two idiots, I'll never recover. To them it's the Ann Southern show as long as I'm there. Only the language is uncensored."

"Well. O.K." Pete was a master of equanimity. He smiled at her and she smiled back.

Right before he fell asleep, he had an involuntary idea for a nutritional balance program, undoubtedly inspired by Bonnie's speculation about the fire. But he mentally filed it under tentative future projects, and then he slept like a baby all night.

HANSEL AND GRETEL

Real Theme: Guilt

After the three Billy Goats Gruff crossed over the bridge to the other side of whatever metaphysical or metaphorical existential pasture they were bent on getting, the troll, Arnold, had little to do with his time. I would run into him at a local bar, where I had taken to dropping in after work at the Emperor's palace, where for the past fifteen years I've been pretending to launder the non-extistent clothes he pretended to wear.

That particular afternoon the troll was bitter at having been duped by the goats: goat meat was his favorite and several times he pounded his beer mug on the table lamenting, "They'd have been tender! Succulent! Delicious!"

He wasn't the ugliest troll I'd ever seen. He had only a few small warts on one cheek, and though his skin color was green, it was a pleasant shade. The frog-like appearance was also due to a lack of chin and the hairless head, though he had one slightly bulging eye. He did have three arms, which worked against his ability to make a good impression visually. His two short stubby legs stuck straight out from the little wooden chair as he sat across from me at the round table.

There were half a dozen tables in the darkened place, each with a small blue or red glass covered in a white waxed net in which a candle burned resolutely. Each table was surrounded by two or three unmatched straight-back wooden chairs. On the walls were paintings of local landscapes done by amateurs. The owner and bartender was a local legend: an ex-prince who abdicated when his father wouldn't let him marry the peasant girl he loved.

As I sat next to the troll I sipped from my empty glass (in which I pretended to have plum wine).

"You know," he said, not looking at me, "those stinking goats weren't the only slime to try to cross my bridge this year."

"Oh?" I said, noticing the deep melancholy expressed in his twisted mouth.

"Yeah. It was back in June. Those two youngsters, Hansel and Gretel, they called themselves. Said their parents abandoned them in the forest. 'What forest?' I said. 'We're right in the middle of the Florida Everglades. Nothing but swamps and a few existential pastures.' God, they were sure a couple of crybabies."

"Well, they were young," I interjected, swirling the imaginary purple liquid in my glass.

"Young? You call mid-twenties young? I don't blame their parents for leaving them. Time they were off on their own. It's a little strange, too, a brother and sister like that."

"It's possible," I said. "Some brothers and sisters are great friends."

He looked at me now with incredulity and suspicion. "Anyway, they said they were lost, and would I direct them back to civilization. They said they had just killed that nice witch, Hortense, who lived in the gingerbread house over by the

143

quicksand bogs. I told them she was the only decent pastry cook in the Northern Hemisphere but they insisted she had wanted to eat them. At least eat the boy and then sell the girl into slavery in the Middle East. Paranoid is what they were. Then they go on and on about their parents ditching them in the forest. Obviously some kind of delusion: I wouldn't be surprised if they hadn't wandered into the swamp on their own.

"They said their father would have let them stay at home as long as they'd have wanted, but he had just remarried a younger woman who wanted the kids out. So, pretending to go on a family outing one Saturday afternoon, they all piled into the Buick and drove into the park. Then the parents abandoned Hansel and Gretel, not far from my bridge, by their descriptions of the place. This happened not once but twice. Can you believe it? The first time the kids stumbled into a ranger who was collecting plant specimens, so they escaped being lost, but the parents did the same thing the very next Saturday, and this time Hansel and Gretel weren't so lucky.

"Now you tell me why two people, actually full grown adults though not independent, would let themselves be put in such jeopardy. I talked to Gretel a bit when they tried to cross my bridge, and she said she actually understood it. She's a psychology student at Miami, I found out later. She said she just wanted to play out the scenario to help the stepmother.

"Now, get this: the stepmother had just put her own parents into a convalescent home. They had enjoyed a long, happy, wealthy retirement there in Miami, and they were both getting sick and senile. It was no financial burden to her to put them away, but an emotional trauma. Gretel thinks that rejecting the two kids of her husband was a mirror image gesture of penance or atonement for incarcerating her own parents."

Here the troll stopped to order another draft. "Rather hard to believe," I said to fill the silence.

144

"Hansel was convinced Gretel was right. He said the step-mother must have had such a guilt complex that only some intense psychoanalysis or therapy would help. He was going to urge her to get professional help when he and Gretel reached home. He said guilt was a terrible thing. The stepmother, forced by natural circumstances or at least societal custom, was forced to do something she really thought was wrong, but only another crime could expiate it. Now she's running around Miami with another guilt complex about child abandonment. Hansel said, 'God knows what she'll do next.'"

"They *are* of age, though," I reminded him.

"Legally, yes. But this isn't a legal issue; it's a moral issue. The legal part comes when Hansel and Gretel murder Hortense. I see it as a cold-blooded premeditated murder in the first degree. They both swear it was self-defense. But where are the witnesses? With the amount of the gingerbread house that had been eaten, not to mention the missing chests of pearls and precious stones, the police would have to be fools not to think the motive was robbery. And the means: her charred remains were right there in the oven, and Gretel had confessed to pushing her in. Self-defense, really! Hortense had been known to eat an elf, or a gremlin or two, but never actually a human being. She was awfully near-sighted: maybe she had taken Hansel and Gretel for elves. But no one will believe that. They'll exonerate the kids. Just wait."

He paused for a moment, then went on. "She was a great gourmet cook, as well. I'm going to miss her. She once fixed me a Beef Wellington that I tasted for days. And what a Chicken Kiev she made for me three years ago on my birthday. Actually we were pretty close. Lately she's been on this breads and pastry kick. I have to watch my weight so I haven't seen that much of her. She showed me the plans for the gingerbread house before she made it. I was quite skeptical and told her, 'The first time it rains the whole thing will collapse into a soggy heap.' But she just laughed at me. I was amazed when the locals started telling me it was finished and standing firm."

Here the troll stopped and with his first two hands cupping his beer mug, he wiped a tear with his third.

"I almost wish she could have eaten those kids."

I said, "What about trying the authorities again? If I were you I'd insist they arrest Hansel and Gretel."

"Are you kidding? The cops treat fairy tale characters like dirt. Or worse, like we don't even exist. Hansel and Gretel are human, and Hortense was a witch. These days you do have to show cause, not like the old days when the humans were just taking over control of existence on the earth, when they burned witches for a Friday night amusement. Of course, we were in control before that so the humans took us seriously. Those were the best times. They'd throw a goat over the bridge as a sacrifice offering before they'd cross it in those days.

"Now, I know you're a man, so I don't want to start laying a guilt trip on you. I know how defensive you people get when someone does that. But . . . you know. Humans have control over everything with their laws and rules now. It's all a big mess. You should have seen what Hortense had to do to get her gingerbread house up to code. And the inspections they're always making on my bridge! They single us out for abuse, but when it comes to protecting our rights, no one's there. And now she's dead.

"It almost makes me happy, the way humans end up when they're old, cast out of their families, locked up in institutions and homes, dying alone with maybe a nurse or an orderly to say goodbye to.

"O.K. Maybe Hansel and Gretel felt they were killing their evil stepmother; she must have seemed like a witch to them. A substitute gesture, a symbol. But why couldn't they just grow up and get out on their own? Find spouses and have their own families—get on with the human scenario? Leave enchanted places alone? They're just jealous anyway because we're ageless and immortal."

I began to perceive that the troll was in his cups now, and I felt sorry for him. I wanted to reach out and pat his shoulder, maybe hold his hand a moment in sympathetic communion. The burden of his grief was so heavy we all could feel it, and periodically the other patrons gave him anxious looks.

"I've got an idea," he said, his eye brightening suddenly. "Come with me."

He grabbed my hand in his third one, the one that sprouted out of the back of his shoulders, and led me out of the bar and down the road at nearly a trot.

"Look here. They can't get away with this. No forest or swamp will be safe if humans are allowed to maraud and plunder at will. We have to get back at them. Not for revenge or restitution, but for a deterrence."

He had now plainly forgotten my origins.

"Here's what we'll do: I know another witch, Vonetta Thompson. She'll throw a spell if we ask the right way, that is, with threats and intimidation. She's not like Hortense, who couldn't ever do enough for you. Anyway, we'll turn those scum humans into alligators or water moccasins. No, too dangerous. Into flamingos. No, too beautiful. Into swamp rats. That's it. Won't be much effort needed since they're so close to it anyway."

We got to Vonetta's home, which was a houseboat with a shingle roof and shingle siding, quite attractive really, and she invited us to sit in her deck chairs on the stern, where mosquitoes began to feast on us.

"How about it Vonetta," said the troll. "Are you going to help us out or do we sink your houseboat and spread a rumor that you're secretly a lesbian?"

She smiled fetchingly, obviously inspired by his approach. "I'd like to help you out, Arnold, but I have no spells left. You know how they regulate us these days. I'd lose my license if they found out it was me who did it."

I noticed how pretty she looked, with her terrycloth shorts and top. She was very fair with blond lashes and eyebrows.

"They'll never find out. They'll all be swamp rats and won't be able to enforce all the rules."

"Besides, the only thing I've been turning people into lately is fawns. There was a brother and sister case not long back . . ."

"Not Hansel and Gretel?" I gasped.

"Oh, no, not them," she mused. "Was it the brother or the sister I had to change? Anyway it's all undone now, so it doesn't matter. But since then fawns are all I've been getting. I have no idea why. Every spell is the same, whether I intended the victim to become a frog or a stone or a tree: fawn is what I get. I guess I'm going to have to go in for a check up."

We left Vonetta's place, dragging our feet. Rather, the troll was dragging his feet: I was just sympathetic and kept quiet out of respect for his pain and loss. I felt the need to protect him.

We reached the fork in the road where we had to part and go our separate ways home.

"Well," he said, "I don't suppose you want to come under my bridge and hang out with me for a while."

"I can't," I said. "I've got to get up at six in the morning to go to work. You know how the human world is. If I don't have the Emperor's pretend clothes clean, all hell will break loose."

"Yeah," he mumbled. "Well, maybe I'll see you around. For a human you're not too bad."

"Thanks," I said. "Maybe I'll drop by and visit you over the weekend."

His one eye looked at me knowingly, and we both suddenly realized we'd never see each other again. Our intimacy was of the one-night stand variety. Now I'd avoid his bar and he'd pretend not to know me if we happened to cross paths. We'd never talk to anyone about what we had shared, and we'd only rarely think about it ourselves.

Pretence: I didn't mind doing my job that way: it's just a job. But I was mightily disappointed in the collapse of the friendship for which I had bent over backwards so far.

THE UGLY DUCKLING

Real Theme: Success

There just has to be a first for everything. Allowing the first black man in the major leagues in baseball was quite a revolution. But when Joan Spenser was allowed to play, even in the minors, it caused a national sensation. And in 1991, the first year she made it in the big leagues, there was only one sports story in all the world.

Joan didn't make rookie of the year at second base, and her .223 batting average was hardly enough to give her hope for stardom, though she did have great wrists. It was only her quick reactions and her deft pivots on the double play that kept her playing regularly on the team. And the time for a woman in baseball had come: in a way she felt like it was just fate. The Tigers were rebuilding that year, and she was the best prospect they had at second base, though a journeyman utility player named Hank "Moose" Fleming was used against knuckleball pitchers on the assumption that Joan was still too green to be put through such humiliation.

Joan was 5' 8", and weighed in at 150 pounds of solid muscle, so, though she was no power hitter due to a lack of upper body strength—attributable to lingering disparities in the upbringings and values of boys and girls—she gave away very little in size to the men around her. She was blonde and blue-eyed as they all preferred, but she had rather large ears and a pointed nose and chin, and in no way could be described as pretty. She did have a good nature and a good sense of humor, and everyone at least tolerated her, even though the management had to give her a private cubicle in the locker room with her own personal shower and bathroom, complete with tampon machine. In fact, she spent so much time in the shower that her teammates gave her the loathsome but obligatory nickname, "The Duck."

Joan had spent three years in the minor leagues after four years playing ball on college teams in Arizona. She was progressed yearly from A to AA to AAA teams, where, amid whirlwinds of media coverage, she had managed to play a superlative second base and to bat around .285. In the minors she had had to come to the park in her uniform and go home to shower and change because they didn't know if she was going to be able to stick it out and there was no sense putting in a whole setup for her if she couldn't make it. Joan went through it all ungrudgingly, in the interest of trailblazing, in the spirit of pioneering.

She was particularly patient with interviews. When she knocked in the winning run, for her first major league RBI in April of '91, the radio announcer Elmo Schultz cornered her after the game, shoved a microphone in her face, and with his annoying style of salting everything with "uh" and always saying "the" with a short "e" even if it did come in front of a vowel, he asked her,

"How does it feel to be in the Major Leagues?"

Joan: "Well, it feels real good. I've worked hard to get here and I'm going to work harder to help this team make a run for the pennant this year."

Elmo: "You really think the Tigers are contenders?"

Joan: "Sure. We have as good a chance as anyone. With our starting rotation led by Archie Chandler and a one-two relief corp with Lefty Russell and Marty Salazar, we have some of the best pitching in the majors."

Elmo: "You had your first Major League RBI tonight, Joan. And it was a game winner. How did that feel?"

Joan: "It felt just great, Elmo. I'm glad I could begin to contribute with my bat so early in the season. I knew I could do it with my glove, but we need as much offense as we can get."

Elmo: "As everyone who's seen you play says, 'Her glove speaks for itself.'"

After a fairly good start, though, her first year was overall an offensive disappointment. She became known as a dead fastball hitter, and soon every pitcher in the league was throwing her nothing but breaking stuff. She always batted near the bottom of the order, and if the game were close in the late innings, the manager, Basil Malone, would always take her out for a pinch hitter and play Moose Fleming at second. This saddened her and had a very negative effect on her ego, but she just worked harder, coming in early to take extra batting practice every day, watching films of herself and of other classic batters and pumping anyone who would talk to her for tips and advice. She was not the only player on the team who wasn't producing runs: the Tigers came in last that year, with a dismal record of 64-98.

She wanted to play winter ball, but the Mexican League was still not ready for women, and she ended up sitting around all winter, nervously waiting for spring training. She worked out to keep in shape and she ran a lot, so when March rolled around she was ready to show what she could do. She could spray hit fastballs just about anywhere she wanted, and she was a good bunter, consistently able to advance the runner by hitting to the right side when necessary. But she just couldn't time a breaking ball and was especially susceptible to inside low balls, often striking out on them once the opposing pitchers got word of it.

Basil, swarthy, short and thin, with black teeth and a slight wall eye, took her aside just before opening day and said, "Joan, you won't see a dozen fastballs all year."

Joan, who had an ace bandage around her right knee, which had been hurting her all winter, said, "I've tried and tried to learn how to hit a curve or slider. I'm not giving up until I get it." She was wearing her hair a tiny bit longer this year and it showed out from under her cap.

"Maybe you should be in the National League. You'd see more fastballs there," said Basil. But then he smiled to reassure her, and he stepped out of the dugout to tell another player something about his swing.

When he returned, they stood again together, watching the practice. Joan said, "I wouldn't like the National League anyway because I'd be stuck hitting right in front of the pitcher all the time, with no DH over there yet. I'd never get any good pitches to hit."

Basil tapped his long graceful fingers on his sagging upper arms, as the crack of a ball on a bat made him turn his face from Joan to the field. "Well," he said, "Keep it up. If you work at it long enough, you'll get the hang of it."

"I know I will." Joan spit in her glove and rubbed the saliva into the pocket. Then she ran out to the outfield to get some practice on pop flies.

Ignoring the superstition of the sophomore jinx, Joan began her second season in the majors full of hope and resolution. She hit two home runs that spring, which yielded her another interview with Elmo Schultz. Elmo was not giving in to popular pressure to exploit her as a curiosity and thus was only interviewing her if she deserved it. Basil noticed her .250 average, and in June he tried her as a lead-off hitter. She had been a good base stealer in college, but they didn't let her do much of it in the minors, for no known reason. Now, she was thrown out five times trying to steal second after walks or singles (mainly because of her bad knee), and though she was good at drawing the walk and getting wood on the ball, her average began to slip, and soon she was back in the rut, getting fooled on curves and sliders. The Tigers finished third that year, though, because of exceptional pitching.

In the off-season the Tigers traded a couple of prospects for the fine established power hitter and free agent, Roger Lenz, who became the immediate clean-up hitter. Also a trade was made for fielders Greg Harrison and Alfred "Spike" Walbrook to bolster the bench. The team was shaping up. Joan practiced double plays with shortstop Freddie Carboni, also out of the farm system, until they could have done it blindfolded.

Joan had to have the cartilage removed from her knee that winter. She started the season and tried to come back from the surgery too fast, reinjuring the knee. She was on the DL until June, really not back to form until late July, and her average was so low by then there was little hope for raising it above .250, as she wished to do. She finished strong at .242 with 31 RBI's and no home runs or stolen bases. She had compensated as much as possible with her fielding, and she had such a high fielding percentage that it was mentioned—even praised—around the league. But a few voices in the media and among the fans began sounding off about getting rid of her because she'd never be a hitter.

The trades for Lenz, Harrison, and Walbrook proved invaluable, and that year they sparked the 1993 Tigers to a 95-67 season, which was good enough for second place to the

Yankees. The starting rotation was solid and experienced now, and Archie Chandler won the Cy Young award with a 21-7 record that year.

When spring rolled around the next year excitement was everywhere the Tigers walked. They were picked to win Division and League, and some oddsmakers were picking them hands down to go all the way.

Joan had the best off-season of her Major League career, working with Roger and Spike, who made her practice hitting curve balls until she began to see movement in every existent phenomenon. Then they put her back on fastballs, and back to breaking balls. Eventually it clicked for her and she hit .350 in spring training. Her knee was finally 100% and she felt a big year coming.

Out of the gate the Tigers put together a winning streak of nine straight and won 15 of their first 20 games. At home they were unbeatable that year, and the crowds of 40,000 to 60,000 that showed up for every home game were indeed the twenty-sixth player. Destiny was on their side: no player had a major injury except Moose Fleming, who was plagued all year by a hamstring, so he was used mainly as a pinch hitter. By the All-Star break Roger Lenz led the league in home runs, RBI's, and slugging percentage, though his batting average was only around .275. Greg Harrison was in the top ten the whole first half of the season, finishing with .341 at the break. Freddie Carboni had matured into a definite base stealing threat, so he batted lead-off. Then came Joan, batting .305, and leading the league in walks for a .459 on-base percentage. With Greg batting third, as DH, Roger clean up, and Spike Walbrook fifth, they could have used high school girls for the rest of the batting order. A young catcher named Rafael Martinez had stolen the show as far as media coverage, though, and he batted a respectable .265 in sixth place in the batting order, as well as having a gun throwing out more base stealers than anyone else in the league, and handling the pitchers with exceptional poise and maturity for a rookie. Basil platooned for the seventh, eighth and ninth positions, just to give everybody some work. Needless to say, spirits and confidence were high, and everyone on the team was having fun.

In July, Joan made the All-Star team as the starting second baseman. She was the media sensation of the event, the most revolutionary thing to hit baseball since the scoreboard. She played six innings of the game, handling four chances flawlessly, and she batted twice in the pitcher's duel, walking once and flying out to right.

Then, as August came on, and the Tigers looked good for going to the World Series, media attention again got to her. All the distractions of interviews, autographs, and invitations to speak at Ladies' Groups must have been responsible for the long agonizing batting slump she experienced. At one point in the slump she was 0-36. Basil benched her. Then the rumor of a romantic entanglement between Joan and Roger Lenz came out in the tabloids, and Joan had even more pressure on her.

As though inspired by adversity she stuck to her story that she and Roger were just friends, as he did, and the rumor-mongers had to look elsewhere for victims. The slump broke by itself in early September. She finally went five for five against Boston, with two doubles and a triple, and, of course, another interview with Elmo. "The slump? Well, it was just one of those things." For the rest of the season she was sizzling and she finished at a career high .297 for the year, also winning a Gold Glove.

The rest is history. The Tigers beat Seattle three straight for the American League championship that year, and beat the Cubs in four straight to win the World Series. No team could touch the '94 Tigers. Joan had played superlative ball and fully deserved the more diminutive Series ring they had made especially for her, as well as the fat multi-year contract her agent negotiated for her that winter.

Joan played on that legendary team until 2005, and though they had many division championships and a few league championships, they never quite managed to go all the way again. Other women began showing up in the majors after Joan's stardom was established, and soon there was even a left-handed relief ace named Shirley Grant. Sexual discrimination wasn't eliminated, but it was a start.

Joan retired at the age of 38 to her horse ranch in Virginia, a contented, wealthy, popular, and happy person, to whom all other women baseball players would be compared. This particular tale shows the utter unpredictability of existence, where nothing, not even failure, persecution, and misery is certain.

ABOUT THE AUTHOR

Margaret Switzer was born in Oakland, California in 1949. She grew up in the Bay Area and studied English and Creative Writing at San Diego State, U.C. Berkeley, and in the San Francisco State graduate Creative Writing program. She lives in Kensington, California.

ABOUT THE CAYUSE PRESS

The Cayuse Indians of northeastern Oregon raised and trained superb horses known for their beauty and reliability. The word later became cowboy slang for his trusted companion. The Cayuse Press is a cooperative through which we may publish, distribute, and promote our work.